My Wine Cellar

Patrick Buttigieg

Revel Barker Publishing

First published 2010 by Revel Barker Publishing

Copyright © Patrick Buttigieg 2010

ISBN: 978-0-9563686-8-3
Revel Barker Publishing
66 Florence Road
Brighton BN2 6DJ
England
revelbarker@gmail.com

This book is sold subject to the condition that it shall not, by way of trade or otherwise, be lent, re-sold, hired out or otherwise circulated without the publisher's prior consent in any form of binding or cover other than that in which it is published and without a similar condition including this condition being imposed on the subsequent purchaser.

Dedication

This book is dedicated first and foremost to my soul mate Yosefa who has never-ending fortitude and dedication towards both me and the restaurant… To my parents Leli & Jane who encouraged me through my apprentice years and who have now fully comprehended why I made the decision to venture away and do my own thing seven years ago… To my good friends Paula and Revel Barker – Revel, who has supported me throughout since the first meal I cooked for him and who came up with the idea of this book and then published it, and Paula, for her professional photography and artwork and for being so patient with Revel and me during our late night discussions over the book… To David and Margaret Procter for their help and support… And to Alex Scicluna, another great friend and business mentor.

We were obviously delighted when, from among more than 1,000 catering establishments in the Maltese islands, our Wine List was, for the fourth time, voted by diners as their favourite.
And we were immensely flattered when customers asked whether they could buy copies to read at their leisure or as gifts for their wine-loving friends.
This volume is also dedicated to those voters and readers.

This wine list, like many of the vintages in it, is priceless! Please check with the current wine list in the restaurant, before ordering.
www.patrickstmun.com

Table of Contents

	Page
Introduction	5
Newcomers	7
Classic Grape Varieties	9
Quick Reference Guide to Our Wine List	15
Verticals	28
Patrick's Reserves	38
Maltese White Wines	46
French White Wines	48
Italian White Wine	52
Spanish White Wines	55
New World White Wines	56
Rosé Wines	60
Maltese Red Wines	62
French Red Wines	66
Italian Red Wines	71
Spanish, Portuguese Red Wines	85
New World Red Wines	87
Sparkling Wines & Champagne	97
Dessert Wines	101
Half & Large Format Bottles	104
Beautiful Memories of the ones that got away	111
Glossary	114

While welcoming you to **Patrick's Tmun**,
*here is a short introduction to our establishment
and a brief overview of our wine list.*

No dish should be better than its ingredients and the best ingredients are usually local.

Freshness is ephemeral and geography expresses itself in the taste of the food, sometimes subtly and at other times profoundly. The food and wines of our islands share a similar motherhood of soil and weather, making for happier culinary marriages than those from dissimilar climates. Chefs who cook with local ingredients season by season, year after year, develop a more complete understanding of their foods than chefs who do not. This understanding can give rise to greater expressions of the food, its preparation, and enjoyment.

Supporting local farmers, cheese makers, fishermen – and especially wineries – helps preserve and promote the foundation of regional cuisines.

After having successfully completed a WSET (Wine & Spirits Education Trust) course last April (2009), I feel even more confident than I used to be. Whether buying quality and value-for-money wines or recommending wines to you, I feel that **Patrick's Tmun** still stands out and will remain as helpful and as dedicated as possible in bringing these wines to your table. And I firmly believe that you will find a great variety of wines on the list to follow.

However, as you may notice, the wine list is heavily focused on wines based on the Shiraz grape variety and Super Tuscan wines. It is by choice and pure passion for these wines, and wines formed from the Shiraz grape, that this list has been compiled in this manner. Our cellar of more than 1,500 bottles encompasses what is perhaps the largest selection of Shiraz based Super Tuscan, as well as rare and hard-to-find bottles from throughout the world that are not available through local retail outlets.

We are also currently investing in various Bordeaux wines *en premiere* that are too young to mention on the wine list.

Red wine is kept at a cellar temperature of 14 degrees and might require a couple of minutes to reach proper serving temperature.

To the best of our knowledge, the wines in our collection have been kept under controlled temperature and humidity since their release. We will replace any corked or spoiled wine of less than 20 years of age. Though we believe our older bottles to be sound, each wine has its own history. For wines of this age, there are no good wines or vintages *per se*, just good bottles.

If you require any assistance in choosing the right wine, please feel free to ask. Our ultimate aim is to ensure all your needs will be met.

We stock Reidel glassware and when possible and necessary we serve our wines in their respective glass.

Top-40 Rated Restaurant,
Award winner 2005, 2006, 2007, 2008, 2009 & 2010

The Best Overall Wine-List,
Award winner 2005, 2006, 2007, 2008, 2009 & 2010

The Best Fine Wine-List,
Award winner 2005

The People's Choice wine award,
Award winner 2007, 2008, 2009 & 2010

The Best Presentation & Accessibility Wine Award,
Award winner 2008 & 2010

Visit our website: www.patrickstmun.com

Let's Give a Big Warm Welcome To This Year's Newcomers...

Along with expanding our verticals list, every year we try to source new and better value for money wines. The wines listed below have been added to this latest version of our wine list and have been selected to complement and enhance our wine list which has been judged tc be the Best Overall wine list in the Maltese islands by The Definitive(ly) Good Guide for the past six years.

Fiano Di Avellino 2008 Mastroberardino, Campania
QR-Light & Crisp

Chablis Premier Cru "Les Vacoupins" 2007
Albert Bichot, Burgundy
Rich & Oaked

Pouilly Fuisse 2007 Albert Bichot, Burgundy
Full & Aromatic

Sauvginon Blanc 2005 Markham, Napa Valley – California
Light & Crisp

Sauvignon Blanc Reserva 2008 Vina Montgras,
Casablanca Valley – Chile
Dry & medium bodied

Chianti Classico Riserva 2004 Castello di Querceto, Tuscany
Dry & earthy reds

Rioja Crianza 2004 Vina Salceda, Rioja
Fruity & medium bodied

Touriga Nacional Reserva 2003 Quinta da Garrida, Dao – Portugal
Fruity & medium bodied

*Malbec "Polo Professional" 2007 La Chamiza,
Mendoza – Argentina*
Dry & medium bodied

*Shiraz Viognier 2006 Domaine Terlato & Chapoutier,
Victoria – Australia*
Medium bodied Shiraz

Palmer, Alter Ego 2002 Margaux, Bordeaux
Cabernet & Cabernet blends

Vidal "Ice Wine" 2007 37.5cl Peller Estate, Ontario – Canada
Dessert wines

*Sauvignon Blanc Botrytis "Noble Iona" 2007
Iona, Elgin – South Africa 37.5cl*
Dessert wines

*Sassicaia Tenuta San Guido 2005 Marchese Incisa della Rocchetta,
Bolgheri,Tuscany – Italy*
Cabernet & Cabernet blends

*Vino Nobile Di Montepulciano Riserva 2001 Fattoria dell Cerro
37.5cl* **Half bottles**

*Sangre De Toro 2006 Torres, Catalunya
37.5cl* **Half bottles**

Veuve Clicquot Rose N/V Ponsardin, Champagne – France
Champagne & Sparkling

*Cordon Rouge, Brut n/v Mumm, Champagne, France
37.5cl* **Half bottles**

Classic International Grape Varieties

By Yosefa Mejlak

In order to appreciate wine it's essential to understand the characteristics different grapes offer and how those characteristics should be expressed in wines. One may drink a glass of wine and simply enjoy its taste but in my opinion it goes much farther than a sip. Wine tasting is an ancient art and a refined understanding of this process will lead to an increase in the pleasure, enjoyment and knowledge of the wines you are drinking. So in order to help you achieve this journey, listed below is a description of the: Classic International Varieties.

CABERNET SAUVIGNON

This undisputed king of red wines is a remarkably steady and consistent performer. At its best, unblended Cabernet Sauvignon produces wines of great intensity and depth of flavour. Its classic flavours are blackcurrant, plum, black cherry and spice. It can also be marked by herb, olive, mint, tobacco, cedar, anise and ripe jammy notes. In warmer areas, it can be supple and elegant, in cooler areas it can be marked by pronounced vegetal, bell pepper, oregano and tar flavour. It is the most dependable candidate for ageing, more often improving into a truly great wine than any other single varietal. With age its distinctive black currant aroma can develop bouquet nuances of cedar, violets, leather or cigar box and its typically tannic edge may soften and smooth considerably. Cabernet Sauvignon has an affinity for oak and usually spends 15 to 30 months in new or used French or American barrels, a process that when properly executed imparts a woody, toasty cedar or vanilla flavour to the wine while slowly oxidizing it and softening the tannins.

CHARDONNAY

Rich is the word that best both describes Chardonnay and explains its popularity. Its aroma is distinct, yet delicate, difficult to characterize, easier to recognize. When well made, Chardonnay offers bold, ripe rich and intense fruit flavours of apples, fig, melon, pear, peach, pineapple, lemon and grapefruit, along with spicy, honey, butter, butterscotch and hazelnut flavours. Its delicacy is such that even a small percentage of another varietal blended into a Chardonnay will often dominate its aroma and flavour. This delicacy also allows Chardonnay to absorb the influences of both vinification technique and appellation of origin. In the Chablis region in France, it is the only grape permitted and it renders a 'crisp, flinty' wine. In the Meursalt appellation, Chardonnay takes on a lush ripe 'fleshy, buttery' quality. Even in quality sparkling wines and French Champagne, it is the major varietal used. California Chardonnay is every bit as variable and possibly even more exciting because of the effusive varietal quality it develops there. In spite of this variety in style Chardonnay is unmistakeable in the mouth because of its impeccable sugar/acid balance, its full body and its easy smoothness.

CHENIN BLANC

This native of the Loire Valley, France has two personalities: at home it's the basis of such famous, long lived whites but on other soils it becomes just a very good blending grape. It is South Africa's most planted grape, though there it is called Steen. Chenin Blanc is arguably the most versatile of all wine grape varieties. Crisp, dry table wines, light sparkling wines, long lived, sumptuous, nectar-like dessert wines and even brandy are all produced in various areas of the wine world, all of Chenin Blanc. No matter the style, a certain floral, honeyed character, along with zesty acidity are the sensory trademarks of well made Chenin Blanc. When conditions are right 'Botrytis Cenerea' (a mould) adds additional complexity and intensity.

GEWURZTRAMINER

Gewurztraminer is one of the most pungent wine varietals, easy for even the beginning taster to recognize by its heady, aromatic scent. Wine texts often repeat that 'gewurz' translates from the German as 'spicy' and 'traminer' as 'early ripener'.

Gewurztraminer can yield magnificent wines, as is best demonstrated in Alsace, France, where it is made into a variety of styles from dry to off dry to sweet. The grape needs a cool climate that allows it to get ripe. Its dark pink colour results in wines coloured from light to dark golden yellow with a copper tone, depending upon the fruit ripeness. Gewurztraminer is quite full bodied, more so than most any other white wine type. In fact, the combination of its strong, heady, perfumery scent, exotic lychee nut flavour and heavy oily texture can be overwhelming and tiring to many palates. There is a slight tendency to bitterness that seems exacerbated by ripeness. Gewurztraminer wines are an excellent match for fresh fruit and cheeses and a good compliment to many simple fish and chicken dishes, especially recipes that include spices.

MERLOT

Merlot is the red wine success of 1990s. Its popularity has soared along with its acreage and it seems wine lovers can't drink enough of it. Because merlot ripens at least a week earlier than either Cabernet variety, it is 'vineyard insurance' when rains are a factor at harvest. The berry of Merlot is relatively thin-skinned and somewhat prone to rot.

While its flavour profile is similar to Cabernet Sauvignon, Merlot tends to be less distinctive and slightly more herbaceous. Overall in both aroma and taste Merlot has slightly lower natural acidity.

Pinot Noir

Pinot Noir the great grape of Burgundy is a touchy variety. It is one of the oldest grape varieties to be cultivated for the purpose of wine making. Great Pinot Noir creates a lasting impression on the palate and in the memory.

Its aroma is often one of the most complex of all varietals and can be intense with a ripe grape or black cherry aroma, frequently accented by a pronounced spiciness that suggests cinnamon, sassafras or mint. Ripe tomato, mushroom and pungent barnyard aromas are also common descriptors for identifying Pinot Noir. It's the most fickle of all grapes to grow and it reacts strongly to environmental changes such as heat and cold spells. Pinot Noir is full bodied and rich but not heavy, high in alcohol, yet neither acidic nor tannic, with substantial flavour despite its delicacy. The most appealing quality of Pinot Noir would be its soft, velvety texture.

When right, it is liquid silk, gently caressing the palate. Pinot Noir does not have the longevity in the bottle of the darker red wines and tends to reach its peak at five to eight years pass the vintage if its not a great wine from Burgundy.

Riesling

One of the world's greatest white wine grapes. The Riesling vine's hardy wood makes it extremely resistant to frost. This variety excels in cooler climates, where its tendency to ripen slowly makes it an excellent source for sweet wines made from grapes attacked by the noble rot, which withers the grapes skin and concentrates their sugar levels. Its wines usually show fresh fruit flavours and a zesty character.

Riesling has the ability to produce wines that run the gamut from bone dry to very sweet but are usually made in dry or semi-dry styles. It has perfumery aromas with peach and honeysuckle notes and can develop a 'petrol' nose as it ages.

SAUVIGNON BLANC

The Sauvignon Blanc grape produces wines of distinction in most areas where it is grown. Sauvignon Blanc is higher in acid and often exhibit melon in the nose and taste. If grown in too cool a climate, it can develop a herbal character in its aromas.

The pure varietal is mainly found in the Loire Valley, France. New Zealand has had striking success with Sauvignon Blanc, producing its own perfumed, fruity style. In the United States, Robert Mondavi rescued the varietal in the 1970's by labelling it 'Fume Blanc'.

Sauvignon Blanc grows well in a variety of appellations. It marries well with Semillon and many vintners are adding a touch of Chardonnay for extra body. The wine drinks best in its youth but sometimes will benefit from short term cellaring.

SEMILLON

On its own or in a blend, this white can age. With Sauvignon Blanc, its traditional partner, this is the foundation of Sauternes and most of the great dry whites found in Graves and Pessac- Leognan, these are rich, honied wines.

Australia's Hunter Valley uses it solo to make a full-bodied white. In South Africa it used to be so prevalent that it was just called 'wine grape'. It can make a wonderful late harvest wine and those wineries that focus on it can make well balanced wines with complex fig, pear, tobacco and honey notes.

When blended into Sauvignon Blanc, it adds body, flavour and texture. When Sauvignon Blanc is added to Semillon, the latter gains grassy herbal notes.

Syrah / Shiraz

Last and foremost stands the Syrah/Shiraz grape variety. This grape is known as Syrah in France and Shiraz in Australia. In the United States it can appear under either name depending on the style of the winery.

The epitome of Syrah is a majestic red that can age for half a century. The grape seems to grow well in a number of areas and is capable of rendering rich, complex and distinctive wines, with pronounced pepper spice, black cherry, tar, leather and roasted nut flavours, a smooth supple texture and smooth tannins.

Syrah is the only grape used to make the famous Rhone wines of Cote Rotie and Hermitage but also forms a back bone of most Rhone blends.

Although cultivated since antiquity, competing claims to the origin of this variety gave credit to it either being transplanted from Persia, near the similarly named city of Shiraz or to being a native plant of France. More than half of the world's total Syrah acreage is planted in France but it is also a successful grape in Australia, South Africa and California. In warmer climates like Australia, the grape produces wines that are sweeter and riper tasting.

In Australia, Shiraz has found a real home, it is the most widely planted red grape variety and is sometimes blended with Cabernet Sauvignon and Mourvedre. It was long used for bread and butter blends, but an increasing number of high quality bottlings are being made, especially from old vines in the Barossa Valley. In cooler climates it often has more pepper and spice aromas and flavours.

In the United States, Syrah rise in quality is most impressive. It appears to have an early drinking appeal of Pinot Noir and Zinfandel.

Quick Reference

Wines served by the glass

Red & white wine by the glass is served from a temperature controlled unit "Vin Au Verre" and can be seen on display at the bar for a wider choice.

WHITE – 150ML
Ramla Valley Antonin 2008
Greco di Tufo 2007

RED – 150ML
Ulysses Syrah 2008
La Segreta Rosso 2006

PORTS – 100ML
10 yr old
20 yr old
30 yr old
Ruby
Junior Tawny

SWEET – 125ML
Nivole Moscato D'Asti
Yalumba Botrytis, Viognier

CHAMPAGNE & BUBBLY – 125ML
Prosecco
MUMM – Cordon Rouge Brut N/V

White Wine – 750ml

Light and Crisp

La Torre Sauvignon Blanc Marsovin 2008

Caravaggio Chenin Blanc 2008

Landini Trebbiano Classico 2008

Muscadet Grande Reserve du Moulin 2006

Domaine du Gouyat 2007

Sancerre La Vigne Blanche 2008

Pouilly Fume 2007

Greco di Tufo 2007

Vermentino La Cala 2008

Marques de Riscal, Sauvignon Blanc 2007

Semillion 2005

35 South S. Blanc 2008

Simonsig Chenin Blanc 2009

Hunters S. Blanc 2008

Matua Valley S. Blanc 2006

Cloudy Bay S. Blanc 2008

Fiano Di Avellino 2008

Sauvginon Blanc 2005

Full and Aromatic

Kessler Gewurztraminer Gran Cru 2001

Jubilee Hugel Reisling 2005

La Dorianne Condrieu 2004

G.T.R Gewurztraminer 2008

The Hermit Crab 2007

Pouilly Fuisse 2007

Pulingy-Montrachet Premier Cru 2007

Dry and Medium Bodied

Cotes du Rhone 2006

Santa Margherita, Pinot Grigio 2008

Rovereto Gavi di Gavi 2008

Le Grillaie 2008

Colomba Platino 2007

Sauvignon Blanc Reserva 2008

The Dry Dam 2007

Clean and Fresh Chardonnays

Caravaggio Chardonnay Marsovin 2008

Isis Chardonnay 2008

1919 Chardonnay Girgentina 2007

Medina Vineyards Chardonnay 2007

Chablis Recolte du Domaine 2007

Lugana Melibeo 2007

La Segreta Bianco I.G.T. 2007

Rawson's Retreat Semillon Chardonnay 2006

Rich and Oaked Chardonnays

Ramla Valley Antonin 2008

Victoria Heights 2008

Cervaro Castello della Sala 2007

Planeta 2005

Gran Vina Sol 2007

Castillo de Molina 2007

Chablis Premier Cru "Les Vacoupins" 2007

Rosé Wines – 750ml

Light and Fruity

Dolcino, Delicata

Medina Vineyards 2008

Les Merles Rose D'Anjou 2008

Rose D'Alghero 2007

Grenache Odyssey 2008

Zinfandel 2007

Santa Digna 2008

Dry and Medium Bodied

Five Roses 2008

Red Wines – 750ml

Light Reds

Beaujolais Villages 2007

Le Orme Barbera D'Asti 2006

Fruity and Medium Bodied

Medina Vineyards 2007

Victoria Heights 2008

Cotes du Rhone Rouge 2005

Chianti Ruffino 2007

Nipozzano Chianti 2005

Vino Nobile di Montepulciano 2005

Rosso di Montalcino Biondi Santi 2007

Rosso di Montalcino La Poderina 2006

Sant Antimo Summus 2000

Terrerare Carignano del Sulcis Riserva 2003
Nero D'Avola, Syrah, Sant' Agostino 2006
Durius Tempranillo 2005
Tri-Centenary Grenache 2002
Bushvine Grenache 2007
Pinot Noir Reserve, Shingle Peak 2007
35 South Merlot 2007
Rioja Crianza 2004
Touriga Nacional Reserva 2003
Antonin Noir 2006

Dry and Medium Bodied
Cheval Franc 2007
Valtellina Sfursat 2001
Gran Sangre del Toro 2005
Malbec "Polo Professional" 2007

Dry and Earthy Reds
La Bernardine Chateauneuf du Pape 2005
Salice Salentino Riserva 2004
Orpheus Etna Rosso 1999
La Segreta Rosso 2007
Simonsig, Pinotage 2006
Chianti Classico Riserva 2004

Cabernet and Cabernet Blends
Marnisi 2006
Melqart 2005
Caravaggio Cabernet Sauvignon 2006

Grand Maitre 2001
Grand Maitre 2002
Grand Maitre 2003
Grand Maitre 2004
Grand Maitre 2005
Grand Maitre 2006
Margaux 2004
Le Petit Mouton Rothschild 2003
Sito Moresco 2006
Sassicaia 2000
Sassicaia 2001
Sassicaia 2002
Sassicaia 2003 1.5L
Sassicaia 2004
Sassicaia 2005
Promis Ca Marcanda 2006
Mas La Plana 2000
Cabo de Hornos 1999
Opus One 1987
Bin 707 1997
Don Melchor 2000
Manso de Velasco 2003
35 South 2008
Castello de Molina C. Sauvignon 2007
Almaviva 2001
Cordillera 2004
Palmer, Alter Ego 2002

Full Bodied Fruity Reds

Grand Vin de Hauteville 2007

Nexus 2006

Chateau La Bonelle 2004

Chateau D'Armailhac 2003

Chateau Clerc Milon 2003

Brunello di Montalcino Pian delle Vigne 2004

Brunello di Montalcino La Poderina 2004

Brunello di Montalcino Tenuta Greppo 1997

Brunello di Montalcino Riserva Poggio al Oro 1997

L'Apparita Merlot 1997

Tignanello 1997

Tignanello 2005

Sassoalloro 2003

Luce 2001

Lamaione 2001

Giramonte 2001

Ripassa Valpolicella Superiore 2006

Amarone della Valpolicella Classico, Tommasi 2001

Amarone della Valpolicella Classico, Zenato 2005

Amarone della Valpolicella Classico, Costasera, Masi 2001

Sagrantino de Montefalco 2003

La Poja 2000

Isola dei Nuraghi 2003

Merlot Planeta I.G.T 2004

Enartis 1999

Full Bodied Dry Reds
Barolo Tortoniano 2004
Barolo Cerequio 2004
Barolo Sperss 1988
Barolo Sperss 1990
Barolo Sperss 1995
Langhe Sperss 1996
Langhe Sperss 1997
Langhe Sperss 1999
Noa 2005

Medium Bodied Shiraz – Syrah
Ulysses Syrah 2008
Bel Syrah 2006
Caravaggio Shiraz 2007
Crozes Hermitage 2005
Planeta Syrah 2005
Magill Estate, Shiraz 1999
Weighbridge Shiraz 2006
Bin 555 – 2005
The Barossa 2005
Shiraz Viognier 2006

Full Bodied Shiraz – Syrah
La Chapelle Hermitage 2002
Le Pavillion Hermitage 1997/1999
Brune et Blonde Cote Rotie 1985
Yalumba Shiraz, Viognier 2005

Three Rivers 1996
Grange 1998
Grange 2000
Grange 2001
RWT 2001
St. Henri 2000
Eight Songs 2000
Stonewell 2002
The McRae Wood 2004
The Armagh 1999
The Armagh 2001
The Armagh 2002
D'Arry's Original 2006
The Dead Arm 2005

Australian Blends
GSM 2007, Peter Lehmann
Mentor 1999
Red Label 2007
GSM 2003, Rosemount
Black Label 2000

LARGE FORMAT BOTTLES

Barolo Cerequio 1998 1.5L
Brunello di Montalcino, La Poderina 1999 1.5L
Vino Nobile di Montepulciano 2001 3.0L
Vino Nobile di Montepulciano Riserva 1999 3.0L
Sassicaia 2003 1.5L
Cordillera 2004 1.5L

HALF BOTTLES – 375ML

White

Recolte du Domaine Chablis 2005
La Vin Blanche Sancerre 2008
Pinot Grigio 2008
Gavi 2008
Carvaggio Chardonnay 2008
Casillero del Diablo, Chardonnay 2007

Red

Melqart 2005
La Bernadine Chateauneuf du Pape 2006
Tortoniano Barolo 2001
Salice Salentino Riserva 2004
Barbera d'Asti 2006
Les Breteches 2006
Amarone della Valpolicella Classico, Costasera 2005
Vino Nobile Di Montepulciano Riserva 2001
Sangre De Toro 2006

Sparkling Wines & Champagne

Brut Mosaique
Brut Yellow Label
Cordon Rouge, Brut n/v Mumm

Champagne & Sparkling

Cassar de Malte 2005

Prosecco di Valdobbiandene Brut

Cava Seleccion Especial Riserva

Pelorus 2001

Mosaique Jaquart Brut Rose

Brut Yellow Label, Veuve Clicquot

Dom Perignon 1996

Cuvee Cristal 2000

Mumm Brut Cordon Rouge

Premiere Cuvee Blanc de Blanc 2001

Veuve Clicquot Rose N/V Ponsardin

Bollinger Grande Annee 1996

Dessert Wines

Caravaggio Moscato 2008 50.0cl

Nivole Moscato d'Asti 2008 37.5cl

Chateau Nairac 1990 75.0cl

Tokaji Azsu 4 Puttonyos 25.0cl

Recioto della Valpolicella 2001 75.0cl

Botrytis Viognier 2006 37.5cl

Chateau d' Yquem 1999 37.5cl

Guze Passito 2001 50.0cl

Recioto Della Valpolicella Classico 2001 50.0cl

Vidal "Ice Wine" 2007 37.5cl

Sauvignon Blanc Bortrytis "Noble Iona" 2007 37.5cl

*Owners' Reserve List

Chateau d'Ampuis Cote Rotie 1999

Grand Vin de Chateau La Tour 1997

Chateau Mouton Rothschild 1993

Chateau Mouton Rothschild 2000

Chateau Margaux 1998

Chateau Angelus 1998

Chateau Palmer 1995

La Turque Cote Rotie 2002

La Landonne Cote Rotie 2002

La Mouline Cote Rotie 2002

Astralis 2001

Opus One 1998

Hill of Grace Shiraz 1996

Hill of Grace Shiraz 1998

Tignanello 1997

Belle Epoque, Brut 1985

Gran Maitre 2001/02/03/04/05/06 1.5L

Isola dei Nuraghi Barrua 2002 1.5L

Bartilot 1997 1.5L

Barolo Brunante 2000 1.5L

Barolo Cannubi 1998 1.5L

Barolo Cannubi 1998 3.0L

Barolo Countacc 1998 3.0L

La Court Barbera d'Asti 1997 3.0L

Barolo Cerequio 1998 1.5L

Barolo Cerequio 2000 3.0L

ALL 2004 BOUGHT *EN PRIMEURS*:

Chateau Lafite Rothschild
Chateau La Tour
Chateau Mouton Rothschild
Chateau Margaux
Chateau Haut Brion
Chateau La Mission Haut Brion
Chateau Cheval Blanc
Chateau D' Yquem 1995
Chateau Petrus

*Please notify the management of interest in these wines as they form a part of the patron's personal collection

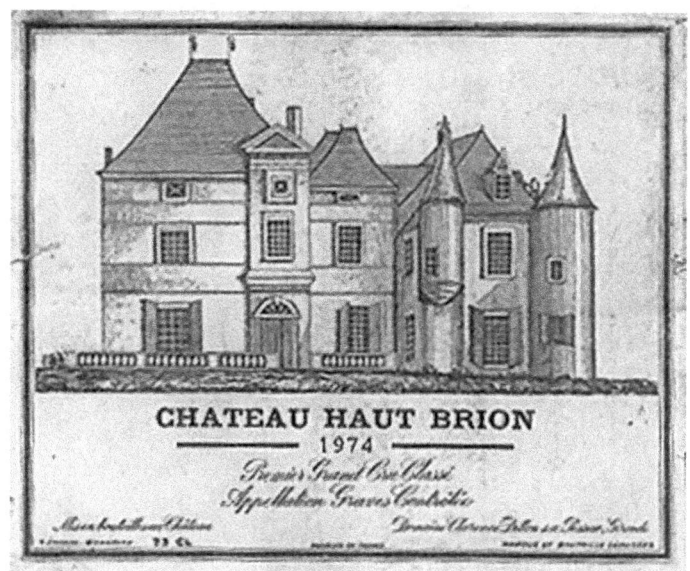

Verticals

In this section I have personally selected some of the finest vintages from their respective winemakers for you to try alongside each other as a vertical tasting.

The idea is simple and works best as a treat for six people or more. Choose your favourite wine from our collection in the verticals section and we will serve you several vintages from that particular winemaker.

Discover how these wines measure up with each other and learn to distinguish certain differences between vintages

GRANGE

GRANGE 1998

Penfolds, South Australia

The 1998 Grange will be legendary. A blend of 97% Shiraz and 3% Cabernet Sauvignon, it tips the scales at a whopping 14.5% alcohol. The inky/purple colour is followed by an extraordinarily intense nose of creme de cassis intermixed with blueberry and floral notes. As the wine sits in the glass, aromas of meat, plums, and cola also emerge. It is a seamless effort with sweet tannin, well-integrated acidity, sensational extract, and layer upon layer of blackberry and cassis fruit that stain the palate and fill the mouth. Its harmony, freshness, and remarkable length (the finish lasts nearly a minute) suggest an all-time classic. Anticipated maturity: 2006-2030.

GRANGE 2000

Penfolds, South Australia

Deep (bright) red crimson colour. On the nose smoky barrel fermented notes hover above a complex base of black liquorice, tobacco, black pepper, exotic spices and plumy, berried fruits. A mouth filling, generous and expansive palate, as expected of this marque. Dark chocolate and plum fruits court a deceptive play of substantial ripe tannins and, at this relatively early stage, provide for a more powerful Grange stamp on the palate than on the nose. Oak plays a supportive role and is perfectly integrated and absorbed. This is a wine of admirable balance and poise, with trademark mid-palate richness.

GRANGE 2001

Penfolds, South Australia

Deep, dark and dense, retaining bright purple hues. The nose is immediately Grange, revealing barrel ferment complexities soaked in dark berried fruits. Vibrant, youthful and lifted, a mix of tightly packed liquorice, freshly tanned leather and dark spices create a poised, controlled and distinctive wine. A rich, full-flavoured and concentrated wine with complex rum/raisin dark chocolate, liquorice, quince paste and dried fruit notes. Prominent, well integrated tannins align with oak (all but soaked up by the fruits) to create a lingering continuum of flavours and tactile persistence. Beautifully balanced, this 100% Barossa wine delivers the expectations demanded of a Grange from this vintage.

GRAND MAITRE

Grand Maitre is a wine dedicated to the Grand Master's of Malta by appointment to the Maltese Association Sovereign Military Order of Malta. Every year it is dedicated to a different Grand Master in chronological order. The nose has rich, chocolaty, blackberry and blackcurrant fruit. There's ripe, velvety fruit on the palate. The oak is not over-evident, but very definitely there. It just feels a touch overblown, but it is in a style that will appeal to many.

ANNATA JUAN DE HOMEDES 2001

Private single estate Ghajn Rihana, Marsovin – Malta

On appearance, the wine has a fairly deep intensity displaying a deep ruby core and a barely noticeable hint of tawny on the rim. Distinguished aromas of a developing nature with a mineral character: tar and flint, complexities of cedar wood, balsamic aromas, mint, liquorice, vanilla and tobacco with a touch of dried fruit. On the palate, abundant unobtrusive tannins and lively acidity define the structure of this wine. A full bodied wine with intense complexities of tobacco, coffee and ripe black fruit, supported by good levels of alcohol and a great length of flavour.Good levels of acidity, pronounced fruitiness, alcohol and tannins guarantee the ageing potential of this wine. Needs further bottle ageing. Drink between 2010 – 2016

ANNATA CLAUDE DE LA SENGLE 2002

Private single estate Ghajn Rihana, Marsovin – Malta

Medium deep intensity with a medium ruby rim and a deep ruby core on appearance.

On the nose it has medium intense aromas of a developing nature with soft and ripe black fruit characteristics: black currants and black cherries with a slight hint of vanilla, coffee and a touch of tropical fruit. Copious levels of smooth and velvety tannins underline the rich fruitiness of prunes, black berries and complexities of tobacco and liquorice on the palate. An overall well-balanced wine, with good acidity, generous alcohol and excellent length. This wine is already approachable but can benefit from a further bottle ageing period of 6 years. Drink between 2009-2015. €450.00

ANNATA JEAN PARISOT DE LA VALETTE 2003

Private single estate Ghajn Rihana, Marsovin – Malta

This vintage is already displaying medium intensity with a deep ruby core and a slight hint of garnet on the rim. Captivating aromas of a developing nature with black fruit characteristics, black cherries, amarena cherries and forest fruit underlined by soft spice aromas: vanilla, cinnamon and nutmeg. Vivacious acidity are evident on the palate and secondary aromas characterize this elegant wine. This medium bodied wine shows a consistent level of silky and ripe tannins. Warm alcohol and intense fruitiness of black currants and black cherries leave a black chocolate finish. A wine that can be drunk now but can keep for 3-4 years (2009 – 2012)

ANNATA PIETRO DEL MONTE 2004

Private single estate Ghajn Rihana, Marsovin – Malta

This vintage also has medium intensity with a medium ruby wide rim and a ruby core. A captivating nose with pronounced aromas of a youthful nature with ripe black fruit: black cherries and forest fruit. As it breathes it shows soft spice characteristics of ginger, white pepper and nutmeg and coffee. Intense sweet rich fruit: amarena cherries and raspberries with very ripe robust tannins on the palate. A medium bodied wine with zesty acidity and alcohol, balanced oak integration with a long and a remarkable finish. This is definitely a wine to keep and that should be drunk between 2011-2018.

ANNATA JEAN L'EVEQUE DE LA CASSIERE 2005

Private single estate Ghajn Rihana, Marsovin – Malta

The 2005 vintage is still young and definitely needs further bottle ageing as their characteristics are still evolving and the wine is still not at its maximum potential.

ANNATA HUGUES LOUBENX DE VERDALLE 2006

Private single estate Ghajn Rihana, Marsovin – Malta

The 2006 vintage is also still quite young and definitely needs further bottle ageing as their characteristics are still evolving and the wine is still not at its maximum potential.

Sassicaia

Sassicaia, Tenuta San Guido, DOC 2000

Marchese Incisa della Rocchetta, Tuscany, Italy

A deep red colour fills the glass, highlighted by streaks of purple. The nose displays an elegant floral fragrance with touches of cassis, black wild berries and cherries. Even in its youth this wine exhibits complex, dry and sapid flavour, wrapped in a woolly blanket of tannin that tickles the palate with a slightly peppery quality; lingering and persistent aftertaste.

Sassicaia, Tenuta San Guido, DOC 2001

Marchese Incisa della Rocchetta, Tuscany, Italy

Beautiful aromas of summer fruits and hints of cream. Then turns to Provencal herbs, such as rosemary. Well-defines Sass. Full-bodied, with sleek, refined tannins and a silky finish. All in finesse. Classy wine. Almost chewy. Reminds me of the excellent 1997, but this is slightly better. Give it time, best after 2008.

Sassicaia, Tenuta San Guido, DOC 2002

Marchese Incisa della Rocchetta, Tuscany, Italy

Very brisk, smooth, seductive nose. Smart, sweet, nose that convinces the taster, in the way of Bordeaux first growth, that only the finest French oak has been used. Gentle, winning texture but pretty expensive. Already a first and satisfying mouthful displaying mild Lafite-like charm. There is quality and vigour here and the wine should have a long life. A good wine to counter 2002's reputation in Italy.

SASSICAIA, TENUTA SAN GUIDO, DOC 2003, 1.5L

Marchese Incisa della Rocchetta, Tuscany, Italy

Ample, sweet and expansive, the 2003 Sassicaia offers generous notes of sweet dark fruit intermingled with notes of spices, herbs, earthiness and smoke in a full-bodied, opulent expression of this wine. It is an outstanding effort for the vintage. Some cellaring is suggested although with air this wine is drinking beautifully right now. Anticipated maturity: 2008-2023.

SASSICAIA, TENUTA SAN GUIDO, DOC 2004

Marchese Incisa della Rocchetta, Tuscany, Italy

The wine is deep in colour with subtle notes of blackcurrant and vanilla on the nose. On the palate intense cassis flavours and precise mineral qualities dominate – ripe, fine grained tannins and firm acidity framework the wine. Poised, very long and elegant. Drink from 2014 but will develop further over the next 20 years plus.

SASSICAIA TENUTA SAN GUIDO 2005

Marchese Incisa della Rocchetta, Bolgheri,Tuscany – Italy

Good deep ruby red in the glass, generous notes of chocolate raisins, some herbs and a little smoke. Medium bodied and very well balanced, lovely mouth-feel with silky tannins. Blackberry on the mid palate, very fresh, lively and fruity with a long & sumptuous finish. This vintage is a stellar effort and rates at 94 Points.

Spersss

Barolo, Sperss 1988
Gaja, Piedmonte, Italy

The Gaja family acquired the 30-acre Sperss vineyard in 1988. The vineyard is located in the Marenca-Rivette area in the commune of Serralunga in the Barolo production zone. The word *sperss* is the Piedmontese term for "nostalgia".

Barolo, Sperss 1990
Gaja, Piedmonte, Italy

A classic vintage of a classic wine. Bottlings of 1990 Barolo of this level are very hard to come by!

Barolo, Sperss 1995
Gaja, Piedmonte, Italy

Power and charm combine in this exotic, black coloured, beautifully perfumed, balanced Barolo. The ageing in barriques gives exquisite results; sweet tannins, fuller body, violet, blackberry, mint, smoke, tar notes and a harmonious finish.

Langhe, Sperss 1996
Gaja, Piedmonte, Italy

In 1996 Angelo Gaja dropped the Barolo appellation in favour of a more relaxed Langhe appellation. This has permitted him to pick his Nebbiolo later, when much riper. He then adjusted the characteristic resulting low acidity by introducing Barbera to the blend. The result is spectacular.

LANGHE, SPERSS 1997

Gaja, Piedmonte, Italy

A superb Sperss with refined aromas of mineral, berries and just a hint of mint.

Full bodied and powerful with chewy tannins and a long berry, cherry and mineral aftertaste. Impressive structure.

LANGHE, SPERSS 1999

Gaja, Piedmonte, Italy

Subtle. Terrific aromas of crushed flowers and berries, with hints of cherries. Full bodied, with silky tannins and a clean, focused finish. A fantastically fine wine.

THE ARMARGH

THE ARMAGH 1999

Jim Barry, Clare Valley, Australia

One of Australia's Classic wines. Totally opaque black purple colour. The nose presents one with a superb sniffing experience – heady aromas of chocolate, marzipan, vanilla and mocha emerge over layers of ripe spicy plums. Mouth filling palate, with dominant flavours of black pepper, plums and spice. Excellent length and persistence. Fine grained soft tannins, yet perfectly in balance, followed by a very long aftertaste of plum, spice and black pepper. Cellar 5-8 years (2006-2015).

THE ARMAGH 2001

Jim Barry, Clare Valley, Australia

It boasts an opaque purple colour in addition to a tremendously rich bouquet of melted liquorice intermixed with scents of camphor, blackberry liqueur, and new saddle leather. Massive and full-bodied, yet impeccably well-balanced, this enormous 2001 should provide riveting drinking for 15+ years. Rating 96 points.

THE ARMAGH 2002

Jim Barry, Clare Valley, Australia

These cuvees are aged 14 months in both French and American oak, and are bottled without filtration. The inky/purple-coloured 2002 The Armagh boasts notes of scorched earth, chocolate, leather, blackberries, and cassis. Its huge body, marvelous integration of acidity, tannin, and alcohol, and stunning finish of 60+ seconds are impressive. While accessible, it will be even better with 1-2 more years of bottle age, and should evolve for 12-15 years plus.

Patrick's Reserves

This section is dedicated to celebrated and prestigious wines which form part of my cherished list of Reserves.

Some of these wines are in their aging process and are too young to drink. A few others form part of Patrick's coveted private collection which, although they are not for sale, are listed here out of sheer pride of owning such rare and distinguished vintages. Finally, there are those of most interest to you; those you can treat yourself to for an evening of fine wine and supreme decadence.

Cote Rotie, Chateau D'Ampuis 1999
Guigal, Rhone

Spices, small soft fruit, and delicate aromas of wood. Tannic and elegant. Aromas of prunes, blackberries and vanilla. Extremely firm tannins mellowed by prolonged ageing in the barrel. Ages at least 20 years.

Cote Rotie, La Landonne 2002
Guigal, Rhone

Deep, saturated red-ruby. Ripe, highly aromatic nose combines raw currant, gunflint and pepper. Then quite tightly wound and still a bit young and subdued, with flavours of crushed currant and fresh herbs.

Cote Rotie, La Turque 2002
Guigal, Rhone

Moderately saturated ruby-red. Captivating aromas of pepper, mocha, wood smoke, bacon fat and spices. Fat and sweet but with a firm edge of acidity. Showing more breadth and texture now than La Mouline. This, too, offers good purity for the vintage, with a strong flavour of dark cherry. Finishes long and sweet, with fine tannins.

Cote Rotie, La Mouline 2002
Guigal, Rhone

Good ruby-red. Aromas of blackcurrant, cherry, liquorice and pepper. Pure and fruity for the vintage but less expansive than usual for La Mouline, with less nuance and depth. Not yet expressive, though.

Chateau Palmer 1995

3ieme Grand Cru Classe, Margaux, Bordeaux

The wines from the 1995 vintage are remarkable for their rich, tannic structure without a trace of astringency. The colour is deep red and very young. This wine has a powerful, rich bouquet featuring slightly jammy blackberry aromas, as well as overtones of leather, gingerbread, and even roasting coffee. The flavour is just as intense, and the tannins provide tightly knit structure. Unusually for a Palmer, the aftertaste is both aromatic and tannic, which gives a good indication of its ageing potential.

Chateau Margaux 1998

1er Grand Cru Classe, Margaux, Bordeaux

The nose is very tight and backward with touches of blueberry and cassis. The palate is tannic with good grip. A certain mineral core with a dash of white pepper sprinkled over the top. Very unapproachable at the moment, this is a more masculine styled Margaux that may need considerable aging to reach its plateau.

Grand Vin De Chateau La Tour 1997

1er Cru Classe, Pauillac, Bordeaux

The wine is of a good standard, without, however, being in the same league as those two wonderfully concentrated vintages 1995 and 1996. Good colours, plenty of fruit, soft texture and reasonable structure are the characteristics of 1997, making well balanced, highly seductive wines which should prove accessible early. The "Grand Vin" of Chateau Latour made from an extremely severe selection of less than half of the total production, confirms authoritatively and with great finesse its exceptional terroir in this technically difficult vintage.

Chateau Mouton Rothschild 1993

1er Grand Cru Classe, Pauillac, Bordeaux

The wine has a fine, garnet colour with a slightly orange tinge. The nose is immediately rich and complete, combining notes of old leather, blackcurrant and humus with torrefaction notes of coffee, mocha, toast and smoke. Fresh on the palate, it shows good structure on fine tannins, pleasantly underpinned by elegant oak and delicious cherry liqueur, cherry pit and caramel notes. The finish lingers on a pleasant impression of oak and vanilla, full of refinement and charm.

Chateau Mouton Rothschild 2000

1er Cru Classe, Pauillac, Bordeaux

The wine has an attractive colour, dark and intense, a vivacious garnet red. The nose is highly expressive, rich and complex, opening on red fruit, blackcurrant and black cherry mingled smoke, coffee, incense and vanilla. Both round and assertive on the palate, showing exceptional potential, it combines the velvet smoothness of well-integrated tannins with the concentration of berry fruit, juicy and crisp. It has no rough edges whatsoever: everything is fused and merged in a perfect union of structure and full, rich, generous flavour. The finish, powerful, explosive and superbly textured, is characteristic of the very finest Mouton vintages.

Chateau Angelus 1998

1er Grand Cru Classe, Saint Emilion, Bordeaux

Plenty of sweet oak and vanilla on the nose. A full bodied youthful wine with tons of tannins with the fruit somewhat forward. A powerful finish. A star performer in this Right bank vintage.

Chateau D'Yquem 1995

1er Grand Cru Classe, Sauternes, Bordeaux, France

Brilliant golden colour. Subtle nose with hints of fruit tart that opens onto honey, dried apricot and almond overtones. Very intense and powerful on the palate with loads of volume. Marmalade and gingerbread flavours evolving into other subtle impressions. A real festival of pleasure! This wine needs time to reveal its full potential.

Tignanello 1997

Marchesi di Antinori, Tuscany

Overall the 1997 harvest has been somewhat less than expected in terms of quantity – but in terms of quality, this is an exceptional vintage, probably even better than the much acclaimed 1990 vintage and one of the greatest of the last fifty years.

Opus One 1998

Robert Mondavi – Mouton Rothschild, California, USA

Opus one fruit comes from the densely planted vineyards that surround the state of the winery in the Oak Ville appellation. It is a blend of 95% Cabernet Sauvignon, 5% Merlot and is aged for 18 months in new French barriques and another 18 months in the bottle before it is released. The nose is powerful full driven complex and oaky, nothing shy or hinting. A Bordeaux complexity amplified to California proportions. On the palate endless layers of semi ripe and mature fruit, immense concentration and winy-ness. It is a full body blockbuster wine. Deep, complex and expressive.

HILL OF GRACE, SHIRAZ 1996

Henschke, Eden Valley, Australia

Very deep crimson in colour. Sweet blackberries, cherries and plums with anise, spicy peppery characters and vanilla aromas. The palate is concentrated and rich with complex flavours, great length and finishes with velvety, silky soft tannins.

HILL OF GRACE, SHIRAZ 1998

Henschke, Eden Valley, Australia

Very deep crimson in colour. A sweet ripe complex exotic nose of prunes, plums, blackberries, cedar and chocolate aromas. A rich sweet succulent palate, complex and well structured with excellent concentration and texture, finishing long with velvety tannins.

ASTRALIS 2001

Clarendon Hills, McLaren Vale, South Australia

The essence of wine, Roman Bratasiuk called it his "Guigal Cote Rotie La Turque". A potentially perfect wine, the inky purple colour offers up and extraordinary nose of sweet creme de cassis and blackberry liqueur, intermixed with smoke, liquorice and espresso. A wine of superb purity and perfect seamless harmony, with incredibly well concealed tannin, alcohol, acidity and wood. This blockbuster brings back memories of Mohammed Ali – "It floats like a butterfly and stings like a bee". It is majestic, large~scaled, and undoubtedly a future legend. Anticipated maturity: 2010-2040.

Belle Epoque 1985

Perriere Jouet, Champagne, France

The outstanding Bohemian style art on the Perrier Jouet can only match the contents of the bottle. Perrier Jouet was established in 1811 in Epernay, the heart of Champagne. The blend consists of 50% Chardonnay, 45% Pinot Noir and 5% Pinot Meunier. The strength of this prestige cuvee is finesse and elegance rather than power of fruit. Creamy style, nutty, bready with yeast elements and a little apple acidity.

Isola Dei Nuraghi, Barrua 2002 1.5L

Agricola Punica, Sardinia

The ultimate embodiment of Carignan. Usually the humble workhorse grape of the Mediterranean here with the help of low yields and old vines is elevated to a veritable superstar of a wine.

Grand Maitre

Grand Maitre is a wine dedicated to the Grand Master's of Malta by appointment to the Maltese Association Sovereign Military Order of Malta. Every year it is dedicated to a different Grand Master in chronological order.

Annata Juan de Homedes 2001 1.5L

Annata Claude de la Sengle 2002 1.5L

Annata Jean Parisot de la Valette 2003 1.5L

Annata Pietro del Monte 2004 1.5L

Annata Jean L'Eveque de la Cassiere 2005 1.5L

Annata Hugues Loubenx de Verdalle 2006 1.5L

Marsovin, Malta

LA COURT BARBERA D'ASTI 1997 3L
BAROLO CEREQUIO 2000 3L
BAROLO COUNTACC 1998 3L
BAROLO CEREQUIO 1998 1.5L
BAROLO BRUNANTE 2000 1.5L
BAROLO CANNUBI 1998 1.5L
BAROLO CANNUBI 1998 3L
BARTILOT 1997 1.5L
Michele Chiarlo from Piemonte, Italy

Maltese Whites

CARAVAGGIO, CHARDONNAY, D.O.K. 2008
Marsovin, Malta

This dry wine exhibits a bright lemon colour with refreshing aromas and flavours of a citrus fruit character of ripe lemons with delicate, floral, aromatic hints, and a crisp level of acidity

LA TORRE, SAUVIGNON BLANC 2008
Marsovin, Malta

Marsovin's Sauvignon Blanc has a very fruity nose reminiscent of melons, tropical fruits and freshly cut grass. It is dry and acidic; crisp yet round to the palate.

1919 CHARDONNAY GIRGENTINA, D.O.K. 2007
Marsovin, Malta

1919 White is produced from four grape varieties; Chardonnay & the indigenous Girgentina, Trebbiano and Vermentino also locally grown and hand picked from selected vineyards. It has a pale straw hue with light golden reflections and a complex bouquet of fresh apple notes married with undertones of tropical papaya.

ANTONIN BLANC, RAMLA VALLEY, D.O.K. 2008
Marsovin, Gozo

Antonin Blanc is produced from selected Chardonnay grapes harvested from the Ramla Valley Estate in Gozo and fermented in new oak barrels for 12 weeks. This wine has a fine balance of acidity, oak and soft buttery flavours.

Caravaggio, Chenin Blanc, d.o.k. Superior 2008
Marsovin, Malta

A dry white wine with aromas reminiscent of apples, peaches and apricots well balanced with refreshing levels of acidity. Ideal to accompany light food dishes including salads, fish, poultry, veal and pork dishes.

Isis, Chardonnay 2008
Meridiana, Malta

Made from Chardonnay grapes, Isis is characterised by fresh tropical fruit flavours.

Landini, Trebbiano Classico 2008
Delicata, Malta

This crisp refreshing full flavoured dry white wine has been produced from hand picked Trebbiano grapes from Friuli in Italy.

Medina Vineyards, Chardonnay Girgentina, i.g.t. 2007
Delicata, Malta

A skillful blend of the Malta grown Chardonnay and the indigenous white grape Girgentina. The crispiness and the fruitiness of the Girgentina complement the fullness and complexity of the Chardonnay perfectly to produce a refreshing dry white wine.

Victoria Heights, Chardonnay i.g.t. 2008
Delicata, Gozo

A soft, fruity full flavoured dry white wine produced entirely from Chardonnay grapes grown in the valley vineyards of Gozo.

French Whites

MUSCADET DE SEVRE ET MAINE SUR LIE, LA GRANDE RESERVE DU MOULIN 2006

Domaine Tourmaline, Loire

The nose develops pleasant aromas of citrus fruits and green apples. The palate is fresh and has good body. Its slightly gaseous aspect is characteristic of wine matured on the lees.

CHABLIS, RECOLTE DU DOMAINE 2007

Joseph Drouhin, Burgundy

A fantastic representative of this great wine from one of the best producers of the area. A wine of intense steely character and prominent acidity.

DOMAINE DU GOUYAT 2007

Dubard, Montravel

The vineyards of the Dordogne can produce some of the most attractive wines in France. Serge Dubard's wine has such crisp gooseberry flavours that it puts many a more expensive wine to shame.

SANCERRE, LA VIGNE BLANCHE 2008

Henri Bourgeois, Loire

A Sauvignon Blanc with a fine persistence and harmony that find their origin in the quality of the terroir and aging on the lees.

POUILLY FUME 2007

Chateau Favray, Loire

The aromatic, floral and smoked nature of the Sauvignon grape variety is the most dominant aspect of this charming wine. It displays its elegance, fruitiness and roundness and is very persistent in the mouth.

POUILLY FUISSE 2007

Albert Bichot, Burgundy

This wine features a pretty green apple bouquet that echoes in the rich, smooth flavours with a certain creamy quality that almost seems to believe the fact that it sees no oak, only stainless steel.

COTES DU RHONE 2006

Guigal, Rhone

Golden clean and brilliant. This is a blend of 55% Viognier, 20% Rousanne and 25% other Rhone varieties. Freshness marked by the distinctive aromas of Viognier. Developing aromas of white flowers, apricot, acacia and white peach. Guigal blend always incorporates a hefty percentage of Viognier. This wine is at its peak, should be drunk now.

JUBILEE HUGEL, RIESLING 2005

Hugel et fils, Alsace

A complex nose of honeyed green apple fruit with developing aromas of gunflint and petroleum, which is an indication of ageing. Light body with medium acidity. It is ready to drink now but not later than early 2015.

KESSLER, GEWURZTRAMINER GRAND CRU 2001
Domains Shlumberger, Alsace

Accessible and harmonious. Full bodied lush, full of vanilla, honey, litchi and spice flavours of an open frame which is very typical of Alsace. Yet with enough structure to keep it focused through the lingering finish. Ready to drink but can keep evolving for about another two years.

CONDRIEU, LA DORIANNE 2004
Guigal, Rhone

Golden hue, plus intensity. Forward aromas of rich honeysuckle, peach, vanilla and banana. Slightly over medium body with good concentration. On the palate the mixed fruit continues and is matched up by great flavours of honey melon, almonds, minerals and butter. Nice and crisp acidity with a remarkable long finish. It is excellent, ready to drink now but can keep up to four more years in the bottle.

CHABLIS PREMIER 1ER CRU, "LES VACOUPINS" 2007
Albert Bichot, Burgundy

The grapes for this wine come from a small vineyard with good exposure and old vines.

Some of the grapes are then fermented in oak while the rest see no oak at all. The final blend offers a rich full-bodied wine whose delicate bouquet occasionally denotes hints of honey suckle.

PULIGNY-MONTRACHET

Premier Cru "Les Perrieres" 2007

Albert Bichot – Burgundy

Pure honey and minerality here, with some oatmeal, this wine has a very linear style. Classically composed, defined, with lots of grippy structure, precise, pure and firm. This is a vigorous wine which somehow still manages to brim with elegance, and overall this is delightfully put together.

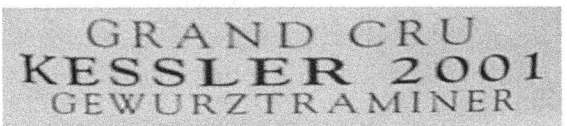

Italian Whites

PINOT GRIGIO 2008
Santa Margherita, Trentino Alto Adige

The clean, intense aroma and dry flavour with pleasant golden apple aftertaste make Santa Margherita Pinot Grigio a wine of great character and versatility.

GAVI DI GAVI, ROVERETO 2008
Michele Chiarlo, Piedmonte

Pale straw with green highlights. The aroma is ample, complex, elegant and persistent with hints of vanilla, chocolate, anise and fresh hay. Dry balanced and fragrant, with silky texture and good length.

LE GRILLAIE, VERNACCIA DI SAN GIMIGNANO 2008
Melini, Tuscany

Bright and pale golden, intense and deep bouquet of flowers and lime tree, underlined by spicy notes of vanilla and nutmeg, pleasant hints of eucalyptus; dry taste, full and harmonious with an aristocratic finish fruit and flint stone.

LUGANA, MELIBEO 2007
Santi, Veneto

A wine of appealing distinctiveness. Releasing crisp, fruity aromas that gradually expand to a rich complexity characteristic only of Lugana. The palate is rounded and generous, and has a wonderfully long, savoury finish.

Cervaro, Castello Della Sala 2007
Marchesi di Antinori, Umbria

A fantastic wine made from Chardonnay and Grechetto. Very fruity and complex on the nose, with hints of vanilla and excellent varietal character. In the mouth it is structured with a very long finish.

Greco Di Tufo 2007
Mastroberardino, Campania

From hill sites at moderate altitudes, where the nature of the terroir exalts the characteristics of the Greco grape. Mastroberardino has dedicated itself to the rediscovery and re-evaluation of this vine along the banks of the river Sabato in Irpinia. The Hellenes imported the variety before the founding of Rome.

Fiano Di Avellino 2008
Mastroberardino, Campania

This light yet interesting wine shows a straw yellow colour with delicate aromas of pear, toasted hazelnuts and citrus fruits. The palate holds splendid acidity, full – bodied and distinct notes of toasted hazelnuts. Pairs well with soups, seafood and white meats.

La Cala, Vermentino Di Sardegna 2008
Sella e Mosca, Sardinia

A light wine with nervous outbursts of marine salt frames heralded fruit, to finish on a long drawn out note of softness.

Colomba Platino 2007
Duca di Salaparuta, Sicily

A fragrant and aromatic wine with an ability to bring the land of Sicily to expression due to an unyielding respect for tradition.

Chardonnay Planeta, I.G.T. 2005

Planeta, Sicily

Deep golden yellow in colour, with rich ripe pear, nectarine and tropical citrus that are structured and well layered with wild flower honey, mineral and toasty vanilla. Never goes over the top, really lovely from beginning to lingering finish. Ready to drink now and over the next couple of years.

La Segreta Bianco, I.G.T. 2007

Planeta, Sicily

70% Greciano, 20% Chardonnay, 10% other varieties, sees no oak. The annual production for this wine is usually 240,000 bottles. La Segreta concludes to be a fresh, modern white showing ripe floral and melon notes. Quite full flavoured.

Spanish Whites

Gran Vina Sol 2007

Torres, Penedes

Chardonnay and Parellada are harmoniously blended after careful fermentation of a percentage in oak barrels, thus retaining the character of each variety. The result is a magnificent, intense wine.

Sauvignon Blanc 2007

Marques de Riscal, Rueda

Expansive, penetrating, intense floral aroma, mingled with a touch of banana. Very pale colour with straw yellow highlights. Very smooth on the palate with a touch of acidity over the whole of the mouth, with no precise fixation.

New World Whites

SAUVIGNON BLANC 2005

Markham, Napa Valley – California

Pale-medium gold reflections with a rich and powerfully aromatic nose of apricot, apple, peach and citrus fruits. On the palate it is full bodied, soft and well-balanced with excellent acidity.

CASTILLO DE MOLINA, CHARDONNAY 2007

San Pedro, Lontue Valley, Chile

Full bodied, well structured, with loads of fruit. Initial strong flavours of ripe peaches, give way to honey and vanilla on the middle palate, with a sweet lasting finish.

35 SOUTH, SAUVIGNON BLANC 2008

San Pedro, Lontue Valley, Chile

A lively fresh and fruity wine with excellent body and structure. Exotic fruit flavours with an elegant citrus finish.

SAUVIGNON BLANC RESERVA 2008

Vina Montgras, Casablanca Valley – Chile

This wine has fresh aromas of green apples, fresh grass and lemon. In the mouth, the wine is bright and full, with clean flavours of tarragon, lemon and green apple.

SIMONSIG, CHENIN BLANC 2009

Stellenbosch, South Africa

An aromatic nose of ripe pears, apples and flowers with a touch of honey. Fresh and intense fruit salad flavours fills the palate with delicious richness on the aftertaste.

HUNTERS, SAUVIGNON BLANC 2008

Marlborough, New Zealand

Ripe passion fruit and hints of gooseberry, this wine is intensely concentrated, rich and racy, finishing with excellent length and crispness.

MATUA VALLEY, SAUVIGNON BLANC 2006

Marlborough, New Zealand

A distinctive and aromatic Marlborough Sauvignon Blanc, delivering bright and lively gooseberry and passion fruit characters with a hint of lime. The palate is well proportioned with refreshing tropical flavours that linger on the seductive finish.

CLOUDY BAY, SAUVIGNON BLANC 2008

Marlborough, New Zealand

Pale straw green in colour and piercingly aromatic, Cloudy Bay shows all the characteristics of a great Sauvignon Blanc. An evocative fusion of fully ripened tropical fruits and freshly cut herbs layered over a base of fresh lime.

RAWSON'S RETREAT
SEMILLON CHARDONNAY 2006

Penfolds, South Eastern Australia

Straw with light honey hues. Fresh tropical fruits with melon and some hints of pineapple combined with creaminess make the nose reminiscent of freshly toasted fruit filled muesli. A wine with generous mouth feel and abundant peach and nectarine fruits, complimented by an ever so slight lemon zest finish.

GEWURZTRAMINER RIESLING, G.T.R. 2008

Rosemount, Mc Laren Vale & Mudgee, Australia

Lively and spicy, the Gewurztraminer gives tropical fruit aromas reminiscent of lychees, whilst the Riesling adds elegance and lifted floral characters. An expressive, medium-dry wine, packed with grapey, fresh fruit flavours.

THE HERMIT CRAB 2007

D'Arenberg Viognier Marsanne, McLaren Vale

The palate is vibrant and expresses plenty of ripe fruit characters with good tightness and control. Flavours range from tropical fruits, nectarine juice, quince, ginger notes with a lovely dry, green melon character. There is plenty of intensity and softness with a hint of lees character to add a little more complexity. The finish has moderate length with good flowery, nutty, mineral notes that complete the wine in a most attractive manner. Chill and enjoy for any occasion.

SEMILLON 2005

Peter Lehmann, South Australia

It's been the freshness of a Riesling and the greater weight of a Chardonnay. The bouquet is clean, developed aromas of lemon flowers, hint of grapefruit and beeswax. A deliciously un-oaked style Semillon to be enjoyed now.

THE DRY DAM 2007 (100% RIESLING)

D'Arenberg, McLaren Vale – Australia

The Dry Dam has a very pale appearance permeated with green tints. Jubilant floral aromas jump out of the glass with a note of citrus blossom and peel. Then spices, green apple, rose petals and fresh cut flower stems. As the wine opens up mineral notes from the soil become more obvious. The palate is youthful, elegantly framed with excellent early-picked flavour ripeness and concentration. It is dominated by green apple, grapefruit, and green melon rind and lime juice with tropical fruit characters coming through. The finish is extremely long and very dry. It's a vibrant, bold, dry style of Riesling which is already extremely appealing to drink.

Maltese – French – Italian Rosé

Dolcino
Delicata, Malta

A deliciously fruity rose wine made using the very latest winemaking technology that captures and maximizes the full fruitiness of the grapes used to produce it.

Medina Vineyards, Grenache, D.O.K. 2008
Delicata, Malta

A fruity, aromatic, rose wine with real character produced entirely from the Malta grown Grenache variety, which is renowned for producing top quality rose wines.

Grenache, Odyssey, D.O.K. 2008
Marsovin, Gozo

This fine Rose' has an intense aroma reminiscent of fresh apple and warm spice, it is medium bodied and is best served lightly chilled accompanying veal, pork and poultry dishes.

Rose D'Anjou, Les Merles 2008
Foucher Lebrun, Loire, France

A gentle medium dry, easy drinking and fruity rose coming from the Loire valley.

Five Roses 2008

Leone de Castris, Apulia, Italy

Obtained from 90% Negroamaro and 10% Black-Malvasia grapes; fruity bouquet; dry and smooth, warm and harmonious flavour.

Rose D'Alghero 2007

Sella e Mosca, Sardinia, Italy

On the nose the wine is full of fruit and texture. On the palate fresh and harmonious.

New World Rose

Zinfandel 2007

Copperidge, California, USA

Lightly sweet and refreshing, the Copperidge Zinfandel has delicate fresh fruit character, accented with enticing spice and floral notes.

Santa Digna, Cabernet Sauvignon 2008

Miguel Torres, Curico, Chile

Fragrant and floral, with a temptingly fruity sensuality. On the palate the wine is voluptuous, with a silky texture and the sort of fresh, fruity body (blackcurrant, cranberry, redcurrant) that only Pacific Cabernet Sauvignon roses can offer.

Maltese Reds

Medina Vineyards, Syrah Grenache Carignan 2007

Delicata, Malta

A skilful blend of three complimentary grape varieties. The fruity robust concentration of the Syrah, the spiciness of the Grenache and the colour and aroma of the Carignan.

Combined they produce this easy drinking, soft, fruity red wine.

Victoria Heights, Merlot D.O.K. 2008

Delicata, Gozo

A full flavoured, robust fruity red wine produced entirely from the Merlot grapes grown in Gozo.

Grand Vin De Hauteville,
Cabernet Shiraz 2007

Delicata, Gozo

A full-bodied fruit packed blend of Shiraz and Cabernet Sauvignon, grapes grown on idyllic Mediterranean island of Gozo.

Cheval Franc D.O.K. Superior 2007

Marsovin, Malta

A medium-bodied wine, with a peppery herbaceous aroma, typical of the Cabernet Franc variety, which dominates this wine.

ULYSSES, SYRAH, D.O.K. SUPERIOR 2008

Marsovin, Gozo

Produced from handpicked Syrah grapes selected from family vineyards in Gozo, found in the vicinity of the picturesque Ramla Valley. A full-bodied ruby red wine that is very delicate on the palate, with soft tannins and fruity aromas reminiscent of raspberries and plums.

MARNISI 2006

Private Estate selection, Marsaxlokk – Marsovin, Malta

Marnisi is a highly tannic, robust red wine expressive of terroir characteristics made with a blend of Cabernet Sauvignon, Merlot, Cabernet Franc, and Petit Verdot from the Marnisi Estate. This wine has deep colour intensity, an aroma of a black fruit character

with oak barrique maturation and complex hints of leather, smoke and spice, giving a longer ageing potential. An overall well balanced local work of art.

BEL, SYRAH 2006

Meridiana, Malta

Made from Syrah grapes, Bel is characterised by soft, silky, prune and peppery spice flavours.

MELQART, CABERNET MERLOT 2005

Meridiana, Malta

Made from an artful blend of Cabernet Sauvignon and Merlot grapes, Melqart is characterised by mellow ripe berry flavours.

NEXUS, MERLOT 2006
Meridiana, Malta

Made from Merlot grapes, Nexus is characterised by tender, ripe, cherry plum flavours.

CARAVAGGIO, SHIRAZ, D.O.K. SUPERIOR 2007
Marsovin, Malta

A medium bodied, dry red wine expressive of terroir characteristics of a black fruit character of blackberry with a complex black peppery and mineral bouquet rounded with soft, ripe tannins.

CARAVAGGIO, CABERNET SAUVIGNON 2006
Marsovin, Malta

A dry, full-bodied, robust red wine with a deep ruby colour, aromas and flavours of a black fruit character of blackcurrants and blueberries rounded with high levels of tannin.

ANTONIN NOIR 2006
Private Estate selection, Marsaxlokk – Marsovin, Malta

Dedicated to Marsovin's late founder Anthony Cassar, affectionately known as Sur Tonin, Antonin Noir is a Private Estate Selection wine blended from Merlot, Cabernet Sauvignon and Cabernet Franc grapes harvested at the Marnisi Estate in Marsaxlokk, the first and the largest in the series of Marsovin's privately owned Estates, intended for the production of premium wines. The fruity characteristics of cherries, blackcurrants and blueberries make this wine enjoyable in its youth while the ageing in French oak barrels gives it a velvety finish on the palate and excellent ageing potential. Antonin is a medium bodied red blend of Merlot, Cabernet Sauvignon and Cabernet Franc varieties. Full fruit flavours of ripe blackberries, cherries and blueberries make this wine very enjoyable in its youth while the backbone and structure provide it with ample ageing potential.

GRAND MAITRE, ANNATA PIETRO DEL MONTE 2004

Private single estate Ghajn Rihana, Marsovin – Malta

This vintage also has medium intensity with a medium ruby wide rim and a ruby core. A captivating nose with pronounced aromas of a youthful nature with ripe black fruit: black cherries and forest fruit. As it breathes it shows soft spice characteristics of ginger, white pepper and nutmeg and coffee. Intense sweet rich fruit: amarena cherries and raspberries with very ripe robust tannins on the palate. A medium bodied wine with zesty acidity and alcohol, balanced oak integration with a long and a remarkable finish. This is definitely a wine to keep and that should be drunk between 2011-2018

French Reds

BEAUJOLAIS VILLAGES 2007
Louis Jadot, Burgundy

Beaujolais Villages is made from a careful selection of various "terroirs" and microclimates, all contributing to make this wine synonymous with charm and conviviality. It has a bright purple colour, a very intense nose, reminiscent of violets and red berries.

COTES DU RHONE 2005
Guigal, Rhone

A fresh, crisp wine with flavours reminiscent of small soft fruit and spices. Full-bodied and elegant, with mellow tannins and an aromatic intensity.

MARGAUX 2004
Calvet, Bordeaux

Margaux area is the widest appellation of Medoc and most well known thanks to Chateau Margaux. Cabernet Sauvignon, Merlot, Cabernet franc and Petit Verdot grown in the gravel carried down from Pyrenees, produce reputed wines for their finesse,

delicacy, sublety characterised by special roundness and softness.

CHATEAU LA BONELLE 2004
Grand Cru, Saint Emilion, Bordeaux

Very studious, meticulous winemaking is behind the reputation of this Chateau guaranteed to make beautifully balanced, vibrantly fruity St Emilion.

CHATEAUNEUF DU PAPE, LA BERNARDINE 2005

Chapoutier, Rhone

A Chateauneuf made from Grenache only, an unusual occurrence in a region that permits up to 13 grape varieties in the blend. This is so because the older vines and superlative wine making still manage to create a wine of great complexity.

CROZES HERMITAGE, DOMAINE DE THALABERT 2005

Jaboulet, Rhone

A full and warm Syrah based wine with ripe raspberry and black cherry aromas. Well structured with liquorice fruit notes on the palate tinged with a helping of black pepper, smoked bacon and cedar.

HERMITAGE, LA CHAPELLE 2002

Jaboulet, Rhone

Every year a wine is born from the vineyards of Paul Jaboulet, a wine with a character that is shaped by nature, the sun and the rain. It was a difficult vintage with strict selection. Very pure dark purple with a hint of red on the rim. Hedonistic aromas of black berries, plums, tar, anise, smoked meat and a handful of coarse ground black pepper and smoke. It is the ultimate old world Syrah with plenty of firm tannin and the necessity acidity that makes it still youthful and has thirty or more years under the belt to go!

Hermitage, Le Pavillion 1997/1999

Chapoutier, Rhone

The merest mention of this wine is enough to make wine lovers raise their eyebrows in respect. It is made entirely from the Syrah grapes grown on the vines that are eighty years old and their wines are destined to live fifty or more years. The colour is between deep purple and garnet red. When first poured it shows cepe mushrooms and red and black fruit, smoke and leather flavours. With deep tannins that are perfectly balanced by depth of fruit flavours that linger seemingly without end on the palate. This wine is as close to perfection as it can get.

Cote Rotie, Cote Brune Et Blonde 1985

Guigal, Rhone

Cote Rotie translates as the "roasted hillside" which sits on the western bank of the, Rhone. Its two hillsides are named "Cote Blonde" and "Cote Brune", so this is where from its name is derived. Its colour is claret on the rim and ruby in the core. Was aged for 24 months in French oak and gives it more the weight of a Grand Cru Burgundy. It is pleasing mainstream wine epitomising Syrah, aiming to be attractive rather than impressive. It is clean, fragrant, ripe, highly typical of Cote-Rotie. There are suggestions of dianthus floral, red plum, cherry and berry flavours. Will cellar for a couple of more years but is at its peak now.

Chateau D'Armailhac 2003

5ieme Grand Cru Classe, Pauillac, Bordeaux

The wine has a deep, intense colour with a purple tint and a concentrated, complex nose, which displays red fruit aromas along with some more mineral notes and fine oak. Well-structured on the palate, its nicely balanced tannins combine with a host of red fruit, spice and vanilla flavours. The long, flavoursome finish holds out the promise of a great future.

Chateau Clerc Milon 2003

5ieme Grand Cru Classe, Pauillac, Bordeaux

The wine has a lovely, deep colour with a carmine tint and a rich, expressive nose, which displays ripe fruit aromas and spicy, oaky notes. Massive on the palate, it builds on developed tannins, revealing liquorice, coffee and blackcurrant flavours. A long, substantial finish with notes of tobacco and roasted coffee rounds off the perfect harmony of this powerful, warmly generous wine.

Le Petit Mouton 2003

2ieme vin de Chateau Mouton Rothschild, Pauillac, Bordeaux

The wine has a fine, deep colour with a violet tint and a highly refined nose that reveals juicy black berry aromas & attractive notes of smoke and toast. The attack is supple and flavorsome, ushering in the crispness of fresh fruit enfolded in forward but already well-rounded tannins. The finish, long and beautifully balanced with a touch of cedar wood, refinement and elegance.

PALMER, ALTER EGO

Margaux, Bordeaux

Alter Ego was born with the 1998 vintage, offering intense, crispy and juicy fruits. It is a spontaneous uninhibited wine, soft and round as soon as it has finished barrel ageing. Its lush aromas and supple tannins make it a wine that can be appreciated in the first years after bottling. The bouquet is first an explosion of dark fruits (blackcurrants, blackberries and blue berries) and spicy notes (cinnamon, pepper and cloves) followed by a rush of woody nuances , cedar, tobacco, leather and discretely the terroir own mineral signature. The attack overwhelms us with the welcoming presence of fully ripened fruit, by the extreme nobility of the velvety tannins and the impeccable ego of an ideal freshness. The wine is full, vigorous and lingers on notes of liquorice and nuts. Last tasted on 01-03-2009 by Chef Patron and it shows that it may be easily stored until 2020.

Italian Reds

Barbera d'Asti, Le Orme 2006
Michele Chiarlo, Piedmonte

Elegant with fine intensity, suggestive of wild berries and mint. Dry full-fruited and well structured.

Barolo, Tortoniano 2004
Michele Chiarlo, Piedmonte

Full, dry, austere and rather harsh when very young, this superb Barolo becomes rich and velvety with age, very harmonious and elegant. It exhibits a distinct bouquet of violets or rose petals, with seductively earthy, slightly musky undertones.

Barolo, Cerequio 2004
Michele Chiarlo, Piedmonte

The Sor☐Cerequio, situated in the communes of La Morra and Barolo, is consistently and universally considered to be one of the greatest and most prestigious crus of the Langhe, sharing this status only with the great Cannubi vineyard, situated entirely in the commune of Barolo.

Sito Moresco 2006
Gaja, Piedmonte

This wine is made from a blend of Nebbiolo, Cabernet and Merlot. Sito Moresco combines complexity and longevity with refinement and accessibility.

BAROLO, SPERSS 1988

Gaja, Piedmonte

The Gaja family acquired the 30-acre Sperss vineyard in 1988. The vineyard is located in the Marenca-Rivette area in the commune of Serralunga in the Barolo production zone. The word sperss is the Piedmontese term for "nostalgia."

BAROLO, SPERSS 1990

Gaja, Piedmonte

A classic vintage of a classic wine. Bottlings of 1990 Barolo of this level are very hard to come by!

BAROLO, SPERSS 1995

Gaja, Piedmonte

Power and charm combine in this exotic, black coloured, beautifully perfumed, balanced Barolo. The ageing in barriques gives exquisite results; sweet tannins, fuller body, violet, blackberry, mint, smoke, tar notes and a harmonious finish.

LANGHE, SPERSS 1996

Gaja, Piedmonte

In 1996 Angelo Gaja dropped the Barolo appellation in favour of a more relaxed Langhe appellation. This has permitted him to pick his Nebbiolo later, when much riper. He then adjusted the characteristic resulting low acidity by introducing Barbera to the blend. The result is spectacular.

Langhe, Sperss 1997

Gaja, Piedmonte

A superb Sperss with refined aromas of mineral, berries and just a hint of mint. Full bodied and powerful with chewy tannins and a long berry, cherry and mineral aftertaste. Impressive structure.

Langhe, Sperss 1999

Gaja, Piedmonte

Subtle. Terrific aromas of crushed flowers and berries, with hints of cherries.

Full bodied, with silky tannins and a clean, focused finish. A fantastically fine wine.

Sfursat Valtellina 2001

Nino Negro, Lombardy

Sfursat is made from a selection of the best grapes of the Valtellina. It owes its name to the classic practice of "forzatura" – already noted in Roman times – which consists of drying bunches to concentrate the juice of the grapes and to increase the sugar content. The resulting wine is particularly robust and alcoholic; it is produced only in the best years in limited quantities.

Chianti 2007

Ruffino, Tuscany

Sangiovese 100%. A wine with a clean, fresh, fruity aroma that is very dry, full of flavour, well balanced, and with a firm after taste.

CHIANTI RUFINA, NIPOZZANO RISERVA 2005
Marchesi de Frescobaldi, Tuscany

A bright intensely coloured wine with a delicate nose, and elements of cherries in alcohol and spices. The palate is characterised from a strong acidity and a tannic element that is present but very refined.

CHIANTI CLASSICO RISERVA 2004
Castello di Querceto, Tuscany

A wine with an intense ruby red colour and with garnet reflections. The bouquet is elegant, full, harmonious and persistent with suggestions of vanilla and raspberry. The palate long and velvety, full, generous and warm.

VINO NOBILE DI MONTEPULCIANO 2005
Fattoria dell Cerro, Tuscany

The most classic and the most famous of wines from Fattoria del Cerro. It has a vivid ruby red colour and good concentration. Intense fragrant aroma with evident fruity notes among which wild black cherry, violet and vanilla. Full balanced flavour with noticeable but discreet tannic component.

BRUNELLO DI MONTALCINO, PIAN DELLE VIGNE 2004
Marchesi di Antinori, Tuscany

Brunello Di Montalcino is a brilliant wine with a lively colour and an intense, persistent, full nose reminiscent of aromatics, woods, small fruit, traces of vanilla and fruity jams, all combined. The wine also has an elegant and harmonic body. Because of its characteristics, Brunello Di Montalcino can withstand lengthy ageing improving with time.

BRUNELLO DI MONTALCINO, LA PODERINA 2004

Tenuta La Poderina, Tuscany

Considered to be something of a modernist because of the use of methods that are strictly speaking not very traditional, such as use of smaller casks instead of the big Slovenian oak vats. Still La Poderina is rated among the best. Maybe just a question of taste.

BRUNELLO DI MONTALCINO,

Tenuta Greppo 1997

Biondi Santi, Tuscany

Wine of great finesse and structure with an intense ruby red colour that lessens with age. Characteristic and intense perfume, delicate and harmonic, with a light scent of vanilla. It is a wine of ample taste, warm and persistent, of great harmony and flavour. Thanks to the perfect characteristics, the long ageing in Slovenian oak casks and the long ageing in the bottle, Brunello Biondi Santi is a wine of great longevity, even over a hundred years.

BRUNELLO DI MONTALCINO RISERVA,

Poggio All' Oro 1997

Castello Banfi, Tuscany

On the famed estate of Castello Banti, where traditional practices are carefully blended with modern technology, rests the single vineyard named La Pievre, from which this spectacular wine originates. Here, with near perfect conditions of climate, soil and sun, the celebrated Brunello grape achieves greatness. Poggio all'Oro is aged for a total of five years, including a minimum of two years in French oak barriques.

L'Apparita, Merlot 1997

Castello di Ama, Tuscany

The "Apparita" vineyard is formed from several small parcels of land particularly rich in clay. The resulting wine has a deep ruby colour with intense varietal character on the nose. Blackberries, cedar, tobacco and smoke come through on the palate. Some dark fruit with hints of coffee. Concentrated and ripe with an excellent finish.

Rosso Di Montalcino, Biondi Santi 2007

Biondi Santi, Tuscany

This wine is made exclusively from Sangiovese grapes, the same variety used for Brunello di Montalcino, which is harvested by hand from younger vines on the property. This wine is ruby red in colour with a pleasantly intense bouquet of wild berry fruits. The palate is velvety and lingering with excellent structure and smooth tannins. "A baby Brunello".

Rosso Di Montalcino 2006

Tenuta La Poderina, Tuscany

A pronounced fragrance, with an evident note of wild berries, and slightly tannic of good persistence. Aged nine months in Slovenian oak casks, followed by three months in the bottle. Can be aged up to five years.

Tignanello 2005

Marchesi di Antinori, Tuscany

80% Sangiovese, 15% Cabernet Sauvignon, 5% Cabernet Franc. Tignanello is produced exclusively from the Tignanello vineyard planted with Sangiovese, Cabernet Sauvignon and Cabernet Franc. The wine is intensely fruity and complex on the nose, with hints of wood, full-bodied rich and complex in the mouth with exceptional structure, and a lengthy finish.

Sangiovese, Manero 2001

Fattoria del Cerro, Tuscany

Manero is made from the estate's finest Sangiovese and is a 100% varietal wine. An inky, impenetrable ruby, its potent aromas of plums, raspberry liqueur, vanilla and sweetness on the nose while the palate is overwhelmed by the rich and solid flavours and a dense, plushy, ripe texture with ample smoky, mineral, and red fruit notes.

Sassicaia, Tenuta San Guido DOC 2000

Marchese Incisa della Rocchetta, Tuscany

Sassicaia is a blend of Cabernet Sauvignon, Sangiovese, and Nebbiolo and was the first Italian wine to successfully establish itself abroad, and is almost universally recognised as the father of the new Italian wine family or simply the Super Tuscan Pioneer. The 2000 shows its class. Loaded with fruit. Rich yet balanced, with lots of jam and plum character. Full-bodied, with round tannins and a silky finish. Exotic. Sassicaia made excellent wine again in a less than easy year.

Sassicaia, Tenuta San Guido DOC 2001

Marchese Incisa della Rocchetta, Tuscany, Italy

Beautiful aromas of summer fruits and hints of cream. Then turns to Provencal herbs, such as rosemary. Full-bodied, with sleek, refined tannins and a silky finish. All in finesse. Classy wine. Almost chewy. Reminds me of the excellent 1997, but this is slightly better. Give it time, best after 2008.

SASSICAIA, TENUTA SAN GUIDO 2002

Marchese Incisa della Rocchetta, Tuscany

Very brisk, smooth, seductive nose. Smart, sweet, nose that convinces the taster, in the way of Bordeaux first growth, thay only the finest French oak has been used. Already a first and satisfying mouthful displaying mild, Lafite-like charm. There is a quality and vigour here and the wine should have a long life.

SASSICAIA, TENUTA SAN GUIDO, DOC 2004

Marchese Incisa della Rocchetta, Tuscany, Italy

The wine is deep in colour with subtle notes of blackcurrant and vanilla on the nose; on the palate intense cassis flavours and precise mineral qualities dominate – ripe, fine grained tannins and firm acidity framework the wine. Poised, very long and elegant. Drink from 2014 but will develop further over the next 20 years plus.

SASSICAIA TENUTA SAN GUIDO 2005

Marchese Incisa della Rocchetta, Tuscany, Italy

Good deep ruby red in the glass, generous notes of chocolate raisins, some herbs and a little smoke. Medium bodied and very well balanced, lovely mouth-feel with silky tannins. Blackberry on the mid palate, very fresh, lively and fruity with a long & sumptuous finish. This vintage is a stellar effort and rates at 94 Points.

PROMIS, CA' MARCANDA 2006

Gaja, Tuscany

A delightful wine, which combines the elegance and suppleness of Merlot and Syrah with the austerity of Sangiovese. This wine can be appreciated from an early age.

SANT ANTIMO, SUMMUS 2000
Castello Banfi, Tuscany

A fragrant bouquet of fruit, oak and spice. Summus is characterised by a rich colour and lively dance of ripe soft fruit flavours. Cabernet Sauvignon, Sangiovese and Syrah compose this poetry in a bottle.

SASSOALLORO 2003
Biondi Santi, Tuscany

The name Sassoalloro, originates from a rocky mass of volcanic origin, The wine is born from grapes normally used for the production of Brunello. After fermentation in stainless steel, the wine is aged in French oak for 14 months and at least 6 months in bottle prior to being released.

LUCE 2001
Luce della Vite, Tuscany

Luce was the first wine ever produced in Montalcino by blending Sangiovese and Merlot grapes. Combining the roundness and suppleness of Merlot with the structure and elegance of Sangiovese seems an obvious idea, but it took two well established winemakers, Lamberto Frescobaldi and Tim Mondavi, to do that in the land of the world renowned Brunello di Montalcino, a wine made strictly from 100% Sangiovese.

LAMAIONE 2001
Marchesi de Frescobaldi, Tuscany

The wine leads with a beautifully limpid, ruby-flecked purple. Intriguing notes of menthol open on the nose, yielding to lush red fruit, cherry in particular, with a soft spiciness, especially cinnamon, infused throughout. The entry is impressive, broad and generous, with superb fruit and an extractive weight that is compelling but not excessive. The lengthy finish flaunts a rich savouriness.

GIRAMONTE 2001
Marchesi de Frescobaldi, Tuscany
The nose exhibits significant complexity, opening to clean-edged wild berry set into a weave of rich spice that privileges black pepper and clove, with nuances throughout of tobacco leaf. It shows seductive, velvet smooth fullness in the mouth, with excellent, sustained progression. Barely noticeable tannins enhance an alcoholic component that is rich but never out of synch. The finish is remarkable for its appealing, creamy texture and for its seemingly endless sapidity.

AMARONE DELLA VALPOLICELLA CLASSICO 2001
Tommasi, Veneto
Produced from the three Valpolicella grape varieties (Corvina Veronese, Rondinella e Molinara) cultivated high on its hillside terraces. The traditional "pergola veronese" method of training the vines is utilized, and only the best and most mature clusters are selected for Amarone. The grapes are placed directly onto small open racks and brought to the open sided building where they are dried by the cool breezes of autumn and winter until the following February.

AMARONE DELLA VALPOLICELLA CLASSICO 2005
Zenato, Veneto
Made from outstanding corvine, rondinella and sangiovese grapes of the Valpolicella Classico zone, in the communes of Sant'Ambrogio, Negrar, Pedemonte, Fumane, San Pietro in Cariano and Marano. After being picked into small, 2.5kg trays, the grapes are cleaned and placed on drying mats for 4 months in dry, well ventilated rooms. In January they are finally crushed, then very slowly fermented on the skins; the wine goes into 300-litre French barrels and Slavonian oak barrels for maturation, followed by a year's ageing in bottle before release. A wine of superb richness and majestic flavours. The exceptional balance of all its components makes it ideal for lengthy cellaring.

Ripassa, Valpolicella Superiore 2006
Zenato, Veneto

As soon as the fermentation of the dried grapes for the Amarone is complete, selected lots of Valpolicella are then "re-passed" on the Amarone pomace, thus initiating a second fermentation which increases slightly the alcoholic content and gives the wine deeper colour, increased extract, and more complex aromas. After 6 months' bottle ageing, the result is a rounded, velvet textured wine with rich, complex aromas of berries and an impressively lengthy finish that seems to linger forever. Ripassa represents one of the most important milestones in Zenato's winemaking evolution.

Amarone Della Valpolicella Classico, Costasera 2001
Masi, Veneto

The Corvina, Rondinella and Molinara grapes that are used to produce this Amarone come from the communes of Marano, Negrar and Sant' Ambrogio in the Classico areas. Amarone is a majestic wine that combines dignity with power and grace.

La Poja 2000
Allegrini, Veneto

Delicious! Dark ruby towards garnet in colour, meduim to full-bodied, with excellent concentration and structure, generous tannins offset nicely by spicy wood and nose matched well by an array of aromas and flavours, including blackberries, chocolate, vanilla and on the long finish generous hints of spicy mint.

Salice Salentino, Riserva 2004
Leone de Castris, Apulia

Wine obtained from 90% Negramaro and 10% black-Malvasia grapes. Ruby red in colour with garnet red reflections upon ageing. Intense, delicate bouquet; dry harmonious and warm flavour.

Etna Rosso, Orpheus 1999
Tenuta Scilio di Valle Galfina, Sicily
The Valle Galfina valley with its volcanic soil, its particular microclimate and low yields produces very high quality wines. The wines of Tenuta Scilio are made exclusively from the vineyards of the family estate, situated 2300 feet above sea level on the slopes of Mount Etna, cultivated organically, combining Sicilian traditions of winemaking with the most modern techniques of vilification. This produces a wine with a complex nose of fruit and perfume, with a taste that is unctuously delicious, suggestive of black cherries, chocolate, leather and cedar.

Terrerare, Carignano Del Sulcis Riserva 2003
Sella e Mosca, Sardinia
Positive vinous tones with strong fruity character emerging from a light woody background. Warm and generous on the palate with soft smooth tannins, ripe fruits and a subtle note of oak.

La Segreta Rosso 2007
Planeta, Sicily
La Segreta takes its name from the forest that surrounds the Planeta family's Ulmo Vineyard in Sambuca di Sicilia. It was here in 1985 that the research began into the merits of Sicilian, Italian and international grape varieties which has been since continued in all the Planeta vineyards. La Segreta Rosso is a blend of the unique Nero D'Avola and other well known international varieties.

Noa 2005
Cusumano, Sicily
A blend of Nero d'Avola grapes, the strongest expression of Sicily, and Cabernet and Merlot grapes evoking the Atlantic coast of France. Vinified and refined separately in small French oak casks, the percentage of the blended grapes varies every year to make up for the variations of the weather in the particular vintage.

SANT AGOSTINO BAGLIO SORIA, NERO D'AVOLA SYRAH 2006
Firriato, Sicily

An intense wine with a deep ruby red colour, beautiful notes of mature red fruits, and an underlying hint of spices conferred by these exceptional grapes. The palate is full of elegant tannins that give it a long, warm persistent finish.

SYRAH I.G.T 2005
Planeta, Sicily

Ruby red with violet undertones. Varietal patterned after the international style more than the French models; reminiscent of intense spices like pepper and cloves. Fig and fig sap scents predominate, and the woodnotes blend into the fruit gathering into a cocoa–like complex aroma. Young tannins and fresh fruit; luscious and supple in texture, with an impact that is lasting. The power of this wine is due to its complexity more than just the tannin.

ISOLA DEI NURAGHI, BARRUA 2003
Agricola Punica, Sardinia

Deep, bright, ruby red in colour. Intensely flavoured and excellently balanced, it is exceptionally long, with rich and satisfying tannins.

SAGRANTINO DI MONTEFALCO, COLLEPIANO 2003
Arnaldo Caprai, Umbria

Densely coloured, almost black ruby red, which develop to garnet with the aging of the wine. An aromatically sensational, intense aroma, with notes of mature fruit and hints of spice and aromas of vanilla transcended from the barriques. The taste is potent, soft and velvety, with an aftertaste that is slightly bitter.

MERLOT, I.G.T. 2004

Planeta, Sicily

Aged for 12 months in French oak barriques (30% of which are new each year) this merlot packs the limit of 15% alcohol. The annual production for this wine is very strict and is not more than 50,000 bottles. The smoky, tarry nose leads to a palate showing bags of lovely rich fruit. Finishes with quite dry tannins and to conclude this wine is a very powerful Merlot with good concentration.

Spanish, Portuguese Reds

GRAN SANGRE DE TORO 2005
Torres, Catalunya Spain
The entire exuberant aroma traditionally found in an intense, ripe red wine, with a sensual background of fine spices in good balance with perfumed notes reminiscent of blackberries. Full, long finish on the palate.

MAS LA PLANA, CABERNET SAUVIGNON 2000
Torres, Penedes Spain
Deep dense cherry colour, with a touch of mahogany. Wonderfully intense bouquet typical of this vineyard: hints of cranberries, cherries and truffles, with an incense-like quality developed during ageing in wood. Full, elegant and pronounced aftertaste, befitting a wine of this quality.

DURIUS, TEMPRANILLO 2005
Marques de Grignon, Duero Spain
An intense fruity flavour with hints of chocolate and spice on the nose and traces of oak which combine well.

ENARTIS 1999
Marques De Grignon, Rioja
A blend of Tempranillo, Syrah, Cabernet Sauvignon and Merlot that spent 18 months in oak. Very attractive ruby colour. A big nose dominated by raspberry fruit and developing aromas of vanilla, leather and sweet spice. It offers finesse, balance and memorable drinking.

TOURIGA NACIONAL RESERVA 2003

Quinta da Garrida, Dao – Portugal

The entire exuberant aroma traditionally found in an intense, ripe red wine, with a sensual background of fine spices in good balance with perfumed notes reminiscent of blackberries.

RIOJA CRIANZA 2004

Vina Salceda, Rioja

A wine with a deep ruby-red colour and aromas of dark berries and vanilla from the oak. It is also velvety-smooth and very elegant.

New World Reds

MALBEC "POLO PROFESSIONAL" 2007
La Chamiza, Mendoza – Argentina
A beautifully intense wine with sweet aromas of berries and plum jam. A period of oak aging gives it an elegant smoky vanilla finish.

CABO DE HORNOS, CABERNET SAUVIGNON 1999
Vina San Pedro, Lontue Valley, Chile
Intense and ripe aromas, spicy flavours blended with wood, coffee and black fruits. Full bodied with good concentration. The wine will benefit from further ageing of 5 to 8 years.

DON MELCHOR, CABERNET SAUVIGNON 2000
Concha y Toro, Puente Alto, Chile
Ripe fresh fruit and berries lead in the nose of this highly aromatic wine. Later, the tobacco, coffee and chocolate come through although they are well integrated with flavours of vanilla. Mature tannins elegantly convey the best expressions of the Puente Alto vines. The pleasant, long finish displays great harmony and balance in this vintage.

MANSO DE VELASCO, CABERNET SAUVIGNON 2003
Torres, Curico, Chile
The Single Vineyard of Manso de Velasco, named after the founder of the town of Curico, is devoted exclusively to the Cabernet Sauvignon that produces this intense and deeply pigmented wine with an extraordinarily rich aroma of ripe fruit. Its aristocratic Cabernet Sauvignon tannins have a majestic, regal structure, heightened by the creamy background of oak from the Nevers forest that is used in its long barrel-ageing.

35 SOUTH, CABERNET SAUVIGNON 2008

San Pedro, Lontue Valley, Chile

Fresh blackberries, with overtones of mint and vanilla. Full bodied and bursting with sweet, ripe berry fruit. Well balanced with good weight and soft tannins.

35 SOUTH, MERLOT 2007

San Pedro, Lontue Valley, Chile

A well structured, medium bodied wine with smooth tannins. Delicate flavours of cherries, sweet spices and chocolate in the finish.

CASTELLO DE MOLINA, CABERNET SAUVIGNON 2007

San Pedro, Lontue Valley, Chile

Firm ripe tannins provide a strong structured wine which will allow for a long aging. Flavours are primarily of very ripe berries, with an underlying spicy character, adding depth and complexity.

ALMAVIVA 2001

Concha y Toro-Rothschild, Puente Alto, Chile

An intense ruby colour, the wine opens on rich, complex aromas of plum, chocolate, tobacco and cassis. On the palate it reveals the presence of mature tannins, elegantly combined with concentrated fruit and a touch of vanilla. The elegant and harmonious finish of this very fine vintage expresses all the character of Puente Alto.

Cordillera 2004
Miguel Torres, Curico, Chile

Intense dark ruby colour, with hints of purple. Warm and dense aromas reminiscent of spices and forests. The elegant palate has silky tannins and notes of fruit over a background of rich vegetal and spicy tones. Barrel ageing has added touches of vanilla and smoke. The varietal character of the old Carihena vines is outstanding in the long and intense aftertaste.

Simonsig, Pinotage 2006
Stellenbosch, South Africa

A youthful, red wine with luscious ripe berry fruit aromas and flavours from mature bush vines.

Opus One 1987
Mondavi-Rothschild, California, USA

Captivating aromas of currant, smoky French oak, coffee and game. Sweet and meaty in the mouth, with lovely texture and suggestions of exotic spices. Opens out nicely on the back half in a way that few of these '87s do; a mouth feel that can only be described as claret-like. A firmly structured wine, with rich, evolved flavours. Finishes with broad, ripe tannins.

Shingle Peak, Pinot Noir Reserve 2007
Matua Valley, Marlborough, New Zealand

The nose is lifted with bursts of fresh, sweet red fruits and spicy oak. The palate is rich in cherries and strawberry fruit intertwined with creamy French oak. Fine, textured tannins give structure and length to this elegant wine.

Tri-Centenary Grenache 2002
Yalumba, Barossa, Australia
The fruit for the Hand Picked Tri-Centenary Grenache is sourced from a single vineyard in the Barossa Valley, affectionately known as 'The Nursery' block. This vineyard has old bush vines that were planted in 1889, making it some of the oldest Grenache vines in Australia.

Bush Vine, Grenache 2007
Yalumba, Barossa, Australia
A Chateauneuf du Pape from Australia, believe it or not. 70-year-old Grenache vines cultivated in the traditional bush method produce this deep and complex fantastic wine.

Bin 707, Cabernet Sauvignon 1997
Penfolds, South Australia
A mouth filling wine with bright, ripe dark berry fruit and tight grained elongated tannins. With great finesse and showing excellent persistence of flavours, the wine's impressive depth and structure give it immense presence in the glass.

St Henri, Shiraz 2000
Penfolds, Barossa & Mc Laren Vale, Australia
A vibrant crimson colour with a purple core. Savoury aromas laced with bay leaf/spice. Some blackcurrant/blackberry aromas show, most likely due to the 9% Cabernet, albeit from warmer climes in a cool year. There are some secondary characters, demi-glace/soy, no doubt from 14mths in large oak vats. A classy young St. Henri – elegance, balance, substance and persistence. Dark fruits with background liquorice and dark spices reflect Barossa and McLaren Vale origins. The palate is tight and defined, yet texturally round and soft, with ripe tannins and no oak interference.

MAGILL ESTATE, SHIRAZ 1999
Penfolds, Adelaide, Australia

An elegant medium weight wine with velvety texture and fine tannins. A sleek contemporary wine that is crafted in the traditional way. The Magill Estate was the original property of Penfolds.

R.W.T, SHIRAZ 2001
Penfolds, Barossa, Australia

RWT draws fruit from 20 to 100 year-old vineyards arcing across the west and north-west of the Barossa Valley, mostly independently grown. The best vineyards produce fruit of voluptuous intensity, ripe tannins, and juicy flavours. The RWT Shiraz has a very seductive style with a plum/blueberry fruit profile and fine ripe tannins underpinned by savoury French oak. The development of Penfolds Red Winemaking Trial (RWT) reflects extraordinary progress in viticulture and winemaking. The two disciplines are increasingly intertwined, as growers and winemakers work together in search of optimum balance, ripeness and flavour.

GRANGE 2000
Penfolds, South Australia

Tasting Notes: Deep (bright) red crimson colour. On the nose smoky barrel fermented notes hover above a complex base of black liquorice, tobacco, black pepper, exotic spices and plumy, berried fruits. A mouth filling, generous and expansive palate, as expected of this marque. Dark chocolate and plum fruits court a deceptive play of substantial ripe tannins and, at this relatively early stage, provide for a more powerful Grange stamp on the palate than on the nose. Oak plays a supportive role and is perfectly integrated and absorbed. This is a wine of admirable balance and poise, with trademark mid-palate richness.

GRANGE 2001
Penfolds, South Australia

Deep, dark and dense, retaining bright purple hues. The nose is immediately Grange, revealing barrel ferment complexities soaked in dark berried fruits. Vibrant, youthful and lifted, a mix of tightly packed liquorice, freshly tanned leather and dark spices create a poised, controlled and distinctive wine. A rich, full-flavored and concentrated wine with complex rum/raisin dark chocolate, liquorice, quince paste and dried fruit notes. Prominent, well integrated tannins align with oak (all but soaked up by the fruits) to create a lingering continuum of flavours and tactile persistence. Beautifully balanced, this 100% Barossa wine delivers the expectations demanded of a Grange from this vintage.

G.S.M. GRENACHE SHIRAZ MOURVEDRE 2007
Peter Lehmann, Barossa, Australia

Very soft and lifted with beautifully integrated complexity showing plum fruits and a touch of dusted cinnamon. This is a medium-weight red wine; rich and spicy, yet seductively smooth. The Grenache gives the palate sweetness; Shiraz adds structural richness and depth, whilst the Mourvedre brings a spicy wildness. The result – a superb blend, ideal for drinking now.

G.S.M. GRENACHE SHIRAZ MOURVEDRE 2003
Rosemount, McLaren Vale, Australia

Aged for 18 months in American oak, this premium McLaren Vale wine typically combines the rich, spicy flavours of Grenache with the opulent fruit of Syrah and the firm structure of Mourverde. The long, perfumed finish with dusty soft tannins lingers in the mouth.

EIGHT SONGS, SHIRAZ 2000

Peter Lehmann, Barossa, Australia

Made from a rare old vine displaying rich plum and chocolate flavours integrated with the softness of French oak.

STONEWELL, SHIRAZ 2002

Peter Lehmann, Barossa, Australia

A fine celebration of great Barossa Shiraz, rich and full bodied with a structure to live for years. Stonewell has extremely limited production.

MENTOR 1999

Peter Lehmann, Barossa, Australia

A blend of Cabernet Sauvignon, Shiraz, Malbec and Merlot of immense flavour with the Cabernet richness on the palate. A wine produced in very limited amounts.

THE MCRAE WOOD, SHIRAZ 2004

Jim Barry, Clare Valley, Australia

Deep red with purple hues, this wine displays generous aromas of dark cherry and menthol with a background of toasty oak. The palate is rich and concentrated showing sweet coconut, oak and dark cherry flavours. The finish is long with firm coating tannins. This wine already has great depth and concentration, but careful cellaring will further enhance it.

RED LABEL, GRENACHE SHIRAZ 2007
Wolf Blass, South Australia

A wine that displays plum and cherry flavours and the inevitable hints of spice.

WEIGHBRIDGE, SHIRAZ 2006
Peter Lehmann, Barossa, Australia

Delightful fruit with a touch of wild spice and dark chocolate. A medium body wine showing good rounded berry fruit and with a soft long finish.

BLACK LABEL, CABERNET SAUVIGNON SHIRAZ 2000
Wolf Blass, Barossa, Australia

Black Label completes fermentation in new American and French oak prior to extended maturation in the same oak. The wine has a beautiful deep purple colour with bright crimson hues. On the nose and the palate the wine exhibits sweet peppermint characters with hints of chocolate, plum pudding and liquorice.

BIN 555, SHIRAZ 2005
Wyndham`s, South Australia

Ripe spicy plum, berry fruit and a hint of pepper coupled with subtle vanillin American oak. This award winning Shiraz is great value for money.

THE BAROSSA, SHIRAZ 2005
Peter Lehmann, Barossa Valley, Australia

This full bodied shiraz from Barossa valley generates an alcohol level of 14%. Its aroma gives scents of liquorice and chocolate and its tannins are evident on the palate. This is one of the better and more affordable shiraz from Peter Lehmann.

D'ARRY'S, SHIRAZ GRANACHE ORIGINAL 2006
D'Arenberg McLaren, Australia

The fruit characters are distinctively d'Arenberg; very red with a savoury spiced plumy fruit character, mulberry, prunes mixed with dark, tarry chocolate notes. As the wine breathes, a punchy array of cranberry, Satsuma plum, fragrant red berry notes and hints of spiced Grenache appear, The wine further develops with liquorish and a potpourri, earthy meaty element with edges of mineral herbaceous notes. The palate is delightfully balanced with fine tannins, just the correct level of oak and zippy acidity. Very controlled, vibrant and poised.

THE DEAD ARM, SHIRAZ 2005
D'Arenberg, McLaren, Australia

A very dark almost black appearance with a dense purple-red hue. The aroma upon opening is very intense with a complex combination of fragrant spices, red fruits, plum dark cherries, cranberry and blueberry notes with a back drop of very fine oaks, liquorice, white pepper, boot-polish and edges of parsley stalks. The taste is rich, gutsy and virile, dominated with red fruits, cherries, plums and dried black olive. The palate is very controlled, tight and has a wonderful liveliness about it. Even the tannins feel cool and silky with mineral grittiness and wonderful acidity. The length is excellent and beautifully pointed with soft red fruit flavours and spice suggests this wine will have great ability to age.

SHIRAZ VIOGNIER 2006
Domaine Terlato & Chapoutier, Victoria – Australia

A deep purple wine with a complex nose, which offers slightly sweet, musky fruits of the forest aromas from the Shiraz, complimented by subtle hints of cinnamon, cloves with notes of honeysuckle and Rose petal from Viognier.

Three Rivers, Shiraz 1996

Chris Ringland, South Australia

Robert Parker described the Three Rivers Shiraz 1996 as "the great Shiraz produced in Australia". This tiny winery called Chris Ringland makes approximately 100 cases per year so we are very lucky to have this gem in stock. The winemaker sources his fruit from 100 year old dry vines from his vineyard on the edge of the Barossa Valley. The low yielding vines produce tremendously concentrated lush ripe fruit giving the wines their opulence and concentrated flavours. The handmade wines typically mature for more than 40 months in hogsheads. It is extremely rare and this is what mostly justifies the price. This Shiraz is monumental; it is a compelling wine of great richness, flavour breadth and length. An inky blue, purple colour is accompanied by extraordinary scents of flowers, black berries, blueberries and cassis as well as hints of espresso roast, truffles, roasted meat and incense. This sexy, beautifully loaded Shiraz should prove to be immortal, it should keep for three decades or more, but who is going to wait that long to unleash the magic?

Sparkling Wines & Champagne

Cassar De Malte 2005
Marsovin, Malta
This prestigious Marsovin wine takes its name from the winemaking family, in keeping with tradition. It is made from high quality Chardonnay grapes harvested from the family's private 15-tumolo estate in Wardija, where there are 7,500 vines. No more than 8,000 bottles are produced from each harvest, and the process takes more than two years, including two fermentations and 15 months in which the bottles are left to lie on lees.

Prosecco Di Valdobbiadene, Brut N/V
Santa Margherita, Veneto, Italy
A sparkling wine with a clean nose, pleasantly fruity, with whiffs of apples and peach blossoms. Delicate and with a balanced taste, it is excellent as an aperitif, or for a celebratory drink.

Cava Seleccion Especial, Riserva Semi Seco N/V
Marques de Monistrol, Penedes, Spain
Semi-dry with balance and fine aromas formed during ageing. Long-lasting bubbles that make it fresh to the palate.

Pelorus N/V
Cloudy Bay, Marlborough, New Zealand
A gorgeously full-bodied toasty blend of Pinot Noir and Chardonnay with richness full of creamy yeast lees characters like baked bread and wine biscuits, hints of white peach and citrus zest and a power that builds to a nutty finish and a long and lingering sweetish aftertaste.

BRUT MOSAIQUE N/V
Jacquart, Champagne, France
A blend of Chardonnay, Pinot Noir and Pinot Meunier. A persistent trail of fine bubbles with a pale golden yellow colour. Aromas of pear and fresh crusty bread.

MOSAIQUE, BRUT ROSE N/V
Jacquart, Champagne, France
Made from 50% Pinot Noir, 40% Chardonnay, 10% Pinot Meunier. Aromas of candied and dried fruits: refined, complex, with good intensity. Refreshing yet firm on the palate with a good integrated fruit expression.

CORDON ROUGE, BRUT N/V
Mumm, Champagne, France
Power, finesse and elegance are the main attributes of this wine. Round and supple with tasty tropical fruits on the palate. This wine is the product of more than 60 crus, with an average of 95% rating on the Echelle des Crus – high among non-vintage wines. This wine's cuvee was blended from a number of selected vintages, including reserve wines, to maintain its house style and depth of flavour. The age of the base wine and the high proportion of Pinots in the blend make it fuller and richer than most N.V. Champagnes.

YELLOW LABEL, BRUT N/V
Veuve Clicquot Ponsardin, Champagne, France
Yellow Label is a perfect example of harmony between delicacy and power. Dominated by Pinot Noir, this wine has a firm structure, rounded with a touch of Pinot Meunier. Nearly a third of Chardonnay gives it the elegance and finesse needed for perfect balance.

VEUVE CLICQUOT ROSE N/V
Ponsardin, Champagne – France

The wine has a luminous colour with radiant rose accents. The nose is elegant and generous, with initial aromas of fresh red fruit, mainly raspberry, wild strawberry, cherry and blackberry, leading to nutty, dried fruits and biscuit notes. The fresh attack is followed by a fruity harmonious sensation on the palate. The wine is perfected balanced in the best Veuve Clicquot style of pink champagnes, combining elegance and flair. The wine works its magic – this delectably full champagne can be enjoyed as a true delicacy. A deliciously fruity wine in early bloom, this is a wonderful aperitif to be shared as a couple or simply with friends.

DOM PERIGNON 1996

Moet et Chandon, Champagne, France

This is the prestige cuvee of the Moet et Chandon house, named after the Benedictine monk who is attributed with the development of blending the three grape varieties that give Champagne an added dimension of fruitiness, finesse and structure.

CUVEE, CRISTAL 2000

Louis Roederer, Champagne, France

Cristal is made according to the strictest criteria, based on a drastic process of selection applying to the vintage, the cru, the village, the grapes and finally the wines. Only Pinot Noir and Chardonnay grapes from the best sites are used in the production of this legendary cuvee.

GRANDE ANNEE 1996

Bollinger Vintage Champagne France

The House of Bollinger produces vintage champagnes only in exceptional years, when the grapes have reached a perfect quality and maturity with a perfect balance between the acids and sugars. Unlike the "Special Cuvee", the denomination "Grande Annee" given to this champagne is produced only from grapes of that particular harvest. The blend of Grande Annee 1996 is made of 70% pinot noir 30% Chardonnay and was produced only from the cuvee.

PREMIERE CUVEE BLANC DE BLANC 2001

Nyetimber, Sussex, England

Nyetimber has single-handedly made English wine respectable. Golden colour, buttery brioche aromas, roasted nut and pineapple flavours, awesome body and length – this is world-class wine. The 1999 is beautifully balanced, rich and elegant wine displaying ripe Chardonnay fruit and fresh underlying acidity.

Dessert Wines

GUZE PASSITO 2001 50CL
Marsovin, Malta

Guze Passito is a naturally sweet, intense and complex red wine produced from partially raisined, locally grown Shiraz grapes. Guze is reminiscent of intense black fruit, chocolate aromas with sweet, spicy, jammy prune flavours. Delicious with cheese, game and chocolate-based dessert. Guze is dedicated to the former Chairman of Marsovin Joseph Cassar affectionately known as Sur Guzi.

CARAVAGGIO MOSCATO, D.O.K. 2008
Marsovin, Malta

A luscious sweet wine with typical aromatic fruit of orange blossom, and intense grapey aromas, with hints of peaches and apricots. It has a refreshing acidity on the palate with good concentration of fruit, structure and balance.

NIVOLE, MOSCATO D'ASTI 2008 37.5CL
Michele Chiarlo, Piedmonte, Italy

An intense, aromatic and fruity wine, suggestive of sage and grapefruit. Clean, light and delicate, with balanced acidity.

CHATEAU NAIRAC 1990 75CL
Barsac, Bordeaux, France

Chateau Nairac is undoubtedly a high quality wine whose rarity makes it less well known than other wines. The wines often display element of orange peel and apricot. 1990 was a classic vintage for Bordeaux sweet wines.

Vidal "Ice Wine" 2007 37.5cl

Peller Estate, Ontario – Canada

Delicate gold colour with an aromatic bouquet of lemon marmalade, carmelized oranges, golden pineapple and a touch of honey. A rich, medium to full-bodied wine with explosive flavours of honey, golden pineapple, star anise and brown sugar and butter. Some say that Canadian ice wine sometimes exceeds the expectations of Bordeaux's finest! You be the judge...

Tokaji Azsu 4 Puttonyos 25cl

Royal Tokaji, Tokaji, Hungary

The three grape varieties that make the wine are Furmint, Harslevelu and Muscat de Lunel. The characteristics are a vivid gold colour with honeyed apricot and orange peel flavours which are uplifted with dramatic acidity.

Recioto Della Valpolicella 2001 75cl

Domini Veneti, Veneto, Italy

A dark ruby red, intense fruity wine, with a fragrant bouquet. The taste is generous, delicate and above all sweet.

Recioto Della Valpolicella Classico 2001 50cl
Allegrini, Veneto, Italy

A delicious red dessert wine. Lovely nose of sweet herbs, bitter cherries and with a touch of caramel. On the palate this is very sweet, but with wonderful exotic flavours and a nice bitterness countering the sweetness. Quite wonderful; gorgeous concentration. Excellent.

BOTRYTIS VIOGNIER 2006 37.5CL
Yalumba, Wrattonbully, Australia

The intense flavours of Viognier have great synergy with the richness of the Botrytis, offering opulent flavours of apricots, peaches and spice. Exotic, luscious, long and alegant, this wine is an experience to be shared.

CHATEAU D' YQUEM 1999 37.5CL
1er Grand Cru Sauternes, Bordeaux, France

Regarded as Bordeaux's' best dessert wine Chateaux D'Yquem has the most glorious, honeyed may blossom nose. Heavenly orange zest flavours instantly shock your taste buds. So rounded, so rich and so tropically luscious. It has become more awesome and certainly at 11 years of age it is stunning!

SAUVIGNON BLANC BOTRYTIS "NOBLE IONA" 2007 37.5CL
Iona, Elgin – South Africa

The nose shows apricot, honey and almonds and on entry the palate is rich and sweet and the wine appears to almost evaporate on your tongue as the wonderful natural acidity balances the sweetness. An overall great and affordable dessert wine from South Africa.

Whites Half Bottles

CHABLIS, RECOLTE DU DOMAINE 2005
Joseph Drouhin, Burgundy
A fantastic representative of this great wine from one of the best producers of the area. A wine of intense steely character and prominent acidity.

SANCERRE, LA VIGNE BLANCHE 2008
Henri Bourgeois, Loire
A Sauvignon Blanc with a fine persistence and harmony that find their origin in the quality of the terroir and aging on the lees.

PINOT GRIGIO 2008
Santa Margherita, Trentino Alto Adige
The clean, intense aroma and dry flavour with pleasant golden apple aftertaste make Santa Margherita Pinot Grigio a wine of great character and versatility.

GAVI 2008
Michele Chiarlo, Piedmonte
A wine with typical hints of citrus fruit, lime blossom and minerals. It is fresh on the palate, fragrant and well balanced. A very elegant wine.

CARAVAGGIO, CHARDONNAY D.O.K. 2008
Marsovin, Malta
This dry wine exhibits a bright lemon colour with refreshing aromas and flavours of a citrus fruit character of ripe lemons with delicate, floral, aromatic hints, and a crisp level of acidity.

Casillero del Diablo, Chardonnay 2007
Central Valley, Chili

Originally from Bordeaux, France, this variety is used to produce wines that, when aged in oak, reach great levels of flavour and aromatic complexity. Fruit and slightly acidic notes particularly tropical, combine with vanilla traces and a toasted feeling derived from the wood.

Reds Half Bottles

Melqart Cabernet Merlot 2005
Meridiana, Malta

Made from an artful blend of Cabernet Sauvignon and Merlot grapes, Melqart is characterised by mellow ripe berry flavours.

Chateauneuf Du Pape, La Bernardine 2006
Chapoutier, Rhone

A Chateauneuf made from Grenache only, an unusual occurrence in a region that permits up to 13 grape varieties in the blend. This is so because the older vines and superlative wine making still manage to create a wine of great complexity.

Salice Salentino, Riserva 2004
Leone de Castris, Apulia

Wine obtained from 90% Negramaro and 10% black-Malvasia grapes. Ruby red in colour with garnet red reflections upon ageing. Intense, delicate bouquet; dry harmonious and warm flavour.

Barolo, Tortoniano 2001

Michele Chiarlo, Piedmonte

Full, dry, austere and rather harsh when very young, this superb Barolo becomes rich and velvety with age, very harmonious and elegant. It exhibits a distinct bouquet of violets or rose petals, with seductively earthy, slightly musky undertones.

Barbera d'Asti, Le Orme 2006

Michele Chiarlo, Piedmonte

Elegant with fine intensity, suggestive of wild berries and mint. Dry full-fruited and well structured.

Les Breteches 2006

Chateau Kefraya, Bekaa Valley, Lebanon

This wine expresses itself through its cherry-red robe with a purplish shade, typical of its youth and character. The perfume of wild flowers, the scent of black cherry compote and ripe cassis, as well as the spicy kirsch aromas, favour the fragrances emanating from a whole botanical garden.

Amarone della Valpolicella Classico Costasera 2005

Masi Veneto

This year's wines are characterized by high acidity levels and a very deep colour, particularly dark and almost completely opaque ruby red. Bright and full bodied on the nose with aromas of preserved cherries and dried plums together with hints of fruits of the forest and cinnamon. Good weight from the alcohol and good structure on the palate, opening out to attractive aromas of cherries and vanilla. The wine has an elegant and long and velvety finish.

Vino Nobile Di Montepulciano Riserva 2001
Fattoria dell Cerro, Tuscany

The most classic and the most famous of wines from Fattoria Del Cerro. It has a vivid ruby red colour and good concentration. It combines intense fragrant aromas which are typical of the Sangiovese grape with evident fruity notes among which wild black cherry, violet and vanilla. Full balanced flavour with noticeable but discreet tannic component.

Sangre De Toro 2006 37.5cl
Torres, Catalunya

The entire exuberant aroma traditionally found in an intense, ripe red wine, with a sensual background of fine spices in good balance with perfumed notes reminiscent of blackberries. Full, long finish on the palate.

Magnums Reds

BAROLO CEREQUIO 1998 1.5L

Michele Chiarlo, Piedmonte

The Sori Cerequio, situated in the communes of La Morra and Barolo, is consistently and universally considered to be one of the greatest and most prestigious crus of the Langhe, sharing this status only with the great Cannubi vineyard, situated entirely in the commune of Barolo.

VINO NOBILE DI MONTEPULCIANO 2001 3L

Fattoria dell Cerro, Tuscany

The most classic and the most famous of wines from Fattoria del Cerro. It has a vivid ruby red colour and good concentration. Intense fragrant aroma with evident fruity notes among which wild black cherry, violet and vanilla. Full balanced flavour with noticeable but discreet tannic component.

VINO NOBILE DI MONTEPULCIANO, RISERVA 1999 3L

Fattoria dell Cerro, Tuscany

The most classic and the most famous of wines from Fattoria del Cerro. It has a vivid ruby red colour and good concentration. Intense fragrant aroma with evident fruity notes among which wild black cherry, violet and vanilla. Full balanced flavour with noticeable but discreet tannic component.

BRUNELLO DI MONTALCINO 1999 1.5L

Tenuta La Poderina, Tuscany

Considered to be something of a modernist because of the use of methods that are strictly speaking not very traditional, such as use of smaller casks instead of the big Slovenian oak vats. Still La Poderina is rated among the best. Maybe just a question of taste.

SASSICAIA, TENUTA SAN GUIDO DOC 2003 1.5L

Marchese Incisa della Rocchetta, Tuscany

Ample, sweet and expansive, the 2003 Sassicaia offers generous notes of sweet dark fruit intermingled with notes of spices, herbs, earthiness and smoke in a full-bodied, opulent expression of this wine. It is an outstanding effort for the vintage. Some cellaring is suggested although with air this wine is drinking beautifully right now. Anticipated maturity: 2008-2023.

CORDILLERA 2004 1.5L

Miguel Torres, Curico, Chile

Intense dark ruby colour, with hints of purple. Warm and dense aromas reminiscent of spices and forests. The elegant palate has silky tannins and notes of fruit over a background of rich vegetal and spicy tones. Barrel ageing has added touches of vanilla and smoke. The varietal character of the old Carihena vines is outstanding in the long and intense aftertaste.

Half Bottles
Sparkling Wines & Champagne

Brut, Mosaique

Jacquart, Champagne, France

A blend of Chardonnay, Pinot Noir and Pinot Meunier. A persistent trail of fine bubbles with a pale golden yellow colour. Aromas of pear and fresh crusty bread.

Brut, Yellow Label

Veuve Clicquot Ponsardin, Champagne, France

Yellow Label is a perfect example of harmony between delicacy and power. Dominated by Pinot Noir, this wine has a firm structure, rounded with a touch of Pinot Meunier Nearly a third of chardonnay gives it the elegance and finesse needed for perfect balance.

Cordon Rouge, Brut N/V 37.5cl

Mumm, Champagne, France

Power, finesse and elegance are the main attributes of this wine. Round and supple with tasty tropical fruits on the palate. This wine is the product of more than 60 crus, with an average of 95% rating on the Echelle des Crus – high among non-vintage wines. This wine's cuvee was blended from a number of selected vintages, including reserve wines, to maintain its house style and depth of flavour. The age of the base wine and the high proportion of Pinots in the blend make it fuller and richer than most N.V. Champagnes.

Beautiful Memories
...of the ones that got away

GRAND VIN DE CHATEAU LATOUR 1970
1er Cru Classe, Pauillac, Bordeaux, France

"Mouth filling, concentrated and still very tannic. Actually I think we could have opened this bottle to celebrate the 25th Anniversary of Tmun, although it was elegant and gorgeous to drink now. Ruby red colour with an amber edge. Lovely aromas of plum berry and mint. Full-bodied, with currant, dried herb character."

GRAND VIN DE CHATEAU LATOUR 1978
1er Cru Classe, Pauillac, Bordeaux, France

"I am resigning myself to this being one of those wines that will never mellow. A forward-looking palate with mahogany core and tawny rim. A very typical '78 nose of pencil-lead, wet sand and some herbaceousness. Still tough on the palate, very tannic and austere. Melted tar and tobacco. Smoky. Very classic Latour. Thanks to Patrick that recommended the AAA prime steer aged Ribeye to balance its dryness."

SASSICAIA, BOLGHERI SUPERIORE
Tenuta San Guido 2000
Marchese Incisa della Rochetta, Tuscany, Italy

"A wine loaded with fruit, concentrated and rich yet balanced, with lots of jammy and plumy character. Full-bodied, with round tannins and a silky finish. Tasting it blind I would have not matched it to the less than favourable conditions they had during the year in Bolgheri due to excessive heat. The company was also up to the occasion."

CROZES HERMITAGE
Domaine De Thalabert 1990 En Magnum
Jaboulet, Rhone, France
"This is a legendary Thalabert, probably the best Jaboulet has ever produced and certainly the best I ever tasted. An interesting nose to open the flight – beef extract, tea and vegetal aromas dominate. There is some classic grilled meat aroma, which soon gave way to hints of charcoaled oak. Quite a tannic palate, but fat and rich, with some forward acidic berry fruit showing. Lovely wine, still on the way up, maybe to the fact that magnums age slower."

LA CHAPELLE, HERMITAGE 1988 EN MAGNUM
Jaboulet, Rhone, France
"Ruby colour with a developed rim, classic nose – cracked pepper, game, and fruit sweetness – fantastic; the palate has excellent weight and balance, a fine structure, firm ripe acidity and a ripe tannic finish. The wine kept changing and improving for the five hours that passed from decanting till the last drop was poured. Tasted even better with food." – *Patrick*

GRANDE ANNEE 1990
Bollinger, Champagne, France
"Bollinger is at the top of its game consistently. Full bodied and rich, pale yellow in colour, very frothy with a constant stream of fine bubbles. Full nutty bouquet; mouth fillingly rich, wonderful flavour length and acidity. Still a lot of life in this bottle. Cheers to Tmun."

Amarone Della Valpolicella Classico 1999

Allegrini, Veneto, Italy

"Calling this wine full bodied is an under statement. The proficient guys at Tmun opened the bottle and decanted this fantastic wine as soon as we ordered it and also gave us recommendation about another wine to keep us busy whilst the Amarone opened up in the decanter. The wine needless to say was memorable." – *Nick Mason*

Barolo, Cerequio 1998 En Magnum

Michele Chiarlo, Piedmonte, Italy

"The fun of magnum bottles besides the ability to respect certain organoleptic characteristics of the wine and allowing it to mature at a more leisurable pace is the enjoyment of a wine when you are in a big party of people. The ceremony of opening and decanting a larger format bottle did increase our enjoyment of the Tmun experience. The quality of the wine and of our company left nothing to be desired.

Langhe, Sperss 1999

Gaja, Piedmonte, Italy

"I waited a year after Patrick's introduction to this wine – at last I savoured a truly fine wine – the colour was intensely beautiful – amber and ruby, the nose very exciting and after waiting a whole hour for the wine to breath, the wine itself was velvety smoothwith superb flavour." – *Ken & Fiona Buddle*

We always like to have your comments on our prestigious wines...
info@patrickstmun.com

Glossary

A

acetic: Wines, no matter how well made, contain quantities of acetic acidity that have a vinegary smell. If there is an excessive amount of acetic acidity, the wine will have a vinegary smell and be a flawed, acetic wine.

acidic: Wines need natural acidity to taste fresh and lively, but an excess of acidity results in an acidic wine that is tart and sour.

acidity: The acidity level in a wine is critical to its enjoyment and livelihood. The natural acids that appear in wine are citric, tartaric, malic, and lactic. Wines from hot years tend to be lower in acidity, whereas wines from cool, rainy years tend to be high in acidity. Acidity in a wine can preserve the wine's freshness and keep the wine lively, but too much acidity, which masks the wines flavours and compresses its texture, is a flaw.

aftertaste: As the term suggests, the taste left in the mouth when one swallows is the aftertaste. This word is a synonym for length or finish. The longer the aftertaste lingers in the mouth (assuming it is a pleasant taste), the finer the quality of the wine.

aggressive: Aggressive is usually applied to wines that are either high in acidity or have harsh tannins, or both.

angular: Angular wines are wines that lack roundness, generosity, and depth. Wine from poor vintages or wines that are too acidic are often described as being angular.

aroma: Aroma is the smell of a young wine before it has had sufficient time to develop nuances of smell that are then called its bouquet. The word aroma is commonly used to mean the smell of a relatively young, unevolved wine.

astringent: Wines that are astringent are not necessarily bad or good wines. Astringent wines are harsh and coarse to taste, either because they are too young and tannic and just need time to develop, or because they are not well made. The level of tannins (if it is harsh) in a wine contributes to its degree of astringency.

austere: Wines that are austere are generally not terribly pleasant wines to drink. An austere wine is a hard, rather dry wine that lacks richness and generosity. However, young Rhones are not as austere as young Bordeaux.

B

backward: An adjective used to describe (1) a young largely unevolved, closed, and undrinkable wine, (2) a wine that is not ready to drink, or (3) a wine that simply refuses to release its charms and personality.

balance: One of the most desired traits in a wine is good balance, where the concentration of fruit, level of tannins, and acidity are in total harmony. Balanced wines are symmetrical and tend to age gracefully.

barnyard: An unclean, farmyard, fecal aroma that is imparted to a wine because of unclean barrels or unsanitary winemaking facilities.

berrylike: As this descriptive term implies, most red wines have an intense berry fruit character that can suggest blackberries, raspberries, black cherries, mulberries, or even strawberries and cranberries.

big: A big wine is a large-framed, full-bodied wine with an intense and concentrated feel on the palate. Most red Rhone wines are big wines.

blackcurrant: A pronounced smell of blackcurrant fruit is commonly associated with certain Rhone wines. It can vary in intensity from faint to very deep and rich.

body: Body is the weight and fullness of a wine that can be sensed as it crosses the palate. full-bodied wines tend to have a lot of alcohol, concentration, and glycerine.

Botrytis cinerea: The fungus that attacks the grape skins under specific climatic conditions (usually alternating periods of moisture and sunny weather). It causes the grape to become superconcentrated because it causes a natural dehydration. Botrytis cinerea is essential for the great sweet white wines of Barsac and Sauternes. It rarely occurs in the Rhone Valley because of the dry, constant sunshine and gusty winds.

bouquet: As a wine's aroma becomes more developed from bottle aging, the aroma is transformed into a bouquet that is hopefully more than just the smell of the grape.

brawny: A hefty, muscular, full-bodied wine with plenty of weight and flavour, although not always the most elegant or refined sort of wine.

briery: I think of California Zinfandel when the term briery comes into play, denoting that the wine is aggressive and rather spicy.

brilliant: Brilliant relates to the colour of the wine. A brilliant wine is one that s clear, with no haze or cloudiness to the colour.

browning: As red wines age, their colour changes from ruby/purple to dark ruby, to medium ruby, to ruby with an amber edge, to ruby with a brown edge. When a wine is browning it is usually fully mature and not likely to get better.

C

carbonic maceration: This vinification method is used to make soft, fruity, very accessible wines. Whole clusters of grapes are put into a vat that is then filled with carbonic gas. This system is used when fruit is to be emphasized in the final wine in contrast to structure and tannin.

cedar: Rhone reds can have a bouquet that suggests either faintly or overtly the smell of cedarwood. It is a complex aspect of the bouquet.

chewy: If a wine has a rather dense, viscous texture from a high glycerin content, it is often referred to as being chewy. High-extract wines from great vintages can often be chewy, largely because they have higher alcohol hence high levels of glycerine, which imparts a fleshy mouthfeel.

closed: The term closed is used to denote that the wine is not showing its potential, which remains locked in because it is too young. Young wines often close up about 12-18 months after bottling, and depending on the vintage and storage conditions, remain in such a state for several years to more than a decade.

complex: One of the most subjective descriptive terms used, a complex wine is a wine that the taster never gets bored with and finds interesting to drink. Complex wines tend to have a variety of subtle scents and flavours that hold one's interest in the wine.

concentrated: Fine wines, whether they are light-, medium-, or full-bodied, should have concentrated flavours. Concentrated denotes that the wine has a depth and richness of fruit that gives it appeal and interest. Deep is a synonym for concentrated.

corked: A corked wine is a flawed wine that has taken on the smell of cork as a result of an unclean or faulty cork. It is perceptible in a bouquet that shows no fruit, only the smell of musty cork, which reminds me of wet cardboard.

cuvée: Many producers in the Rhone Valley produce special, deluxe lots of wine or a lot of wine from a specific grape variety that they bottle separately. These lots are often referred to as cuvees.

D

decadent: If you are an ice cream and chocolate lover, you know the feeling of eating a huge sundae of rich vanilla ice cream lavished with hot fudge and real whipped cream. If you are a wine enthusiast, a wine loaded with opulent, even unctuous layers of fruit, with a huge bouquet, and a plump, luxurious texture can be said to be decadent.

deep: Essentially the same as concentrated, expressing the fact that the wine is rich, full of extract, and mouth filling.

delicate: As this word implies, delicate wines are light, subtle, understated wines that are prized for their shyness rather than for an extroverted, robust character. White wines are usually more delicate than red wines. Few Rhone red wines can correctly be called delicate.

demi-muid: 650-liter Burgundy barrels which are essentially the equivalent of three regular barrels.

diffuse: Wines that smell and taste unstructured and unfocused are said to be diffuse. When red wines are served at too warm a temperature they often become diffuse.

double decanting: This is done by first decanting the wine into a decanter and then rinsing the original bottle out with non-chlorinated water and then immediately repouring the wine from the decanter back into the bottle. It varies with the wine as to how long you cork it.

dumb: A dumb wine is also a closed wine, but the term dumb is used more pejoratively. Closed wines may need only time to reveal their richness and intensity. Dumb wines may never get any better.

E

earthy: May be used in both a negative and a positive sense; however, I prefer to use earthy to denote a positive aroma of fresh, rich, clean soil. Earthy is a more intense smell than woody or truffle scents.

elegant: Although more white wines than red are described as being elegant, lighter-styled, graceful, balance red wines can be elegant.

extract: This is everything in a wine besides water, sugar, alcohol, and acidity.

exuberant: Like extroverted, somewhat hyper people, wines too can be gushing with fruit and seem nervous and intensely vigorous.

F

fat: When the Rhone has an exceptionally hot year for its crop and the wines attain a super sort of maturity, they are often quite rich and concentrated, with low to average acidity. Often such wines are said to be fat, which is a prized commodity. If they become too fat, that is a flaw and they are then called flabby.

flabby: A wine that is too fat or obese is a flabby wine. Flabby wines lack structure and are heavy to taste.

fleshy: Fleshy is a synonym for chewy, meaty, or beefy. It denotes that the wine has a lot of body, alcohol, and extract, and usually a high glycerin content. Chateauneuf-du-Pape and Hermitage are particularly fleshy wines.

floral: Wines made from the Muscat or Viognier grape have a flowery component, and occasionally a red wine will have a floral scent.

focused: Both a fine wine's bouquet and flavour should be focused. Focused simply means that the scents, aromas, and flavours are precise and clearly delineated. If they are not, the wine is like an out-of-focus picture-diffuse, hazy, and possibly problematic.

forward: An adjective used to describe wines that are (1) delicious, evolved, and close to maturity, (2) wines that border on being flamboyant or ostentatious, or (3) unusually evolved and/or quickly maturing wines.

foudre: Large oak barrels that vary enormously in size but are significantly larger than the normal oak barrel used in Bordeaux or the piece used in Burgundy. They are widely used in the Rhone Valley.

fresh: Freshness in both young and old wines is a welcome and pleasing component. A wine is said to be fresh when it is lively and cleanly made. The opposite of fresh is stale.

fruity: A very good wine should have enough concentration of fruit so that it can be said to be fruity. Fortunately, the best wines will have more than just a fruity personality.

full-bodied: Wines rich in extract, alcohol, and glycerin are full-bodied wines. Most Rhone wines are full-bodied.

G

garrigue: In the southern Rhone Valley and Provence, this is the landscape of small slopes and plateaus. This Provencal word applies to these windswept hilltops/slopes inhabited by scrub-brush and Provencal herb outcroppings. The smell of garrigue is often attributed to southern Rhone Valley wines. Suggesting more than the smell of herbes de Provence, it encompasses an earthy/herbal concoction of varying degrees of intensity.

green: Green wines are wines made from underripe grapes; they lack richness and generosity as well as having a vegetal character. Green wines are infrequently made in the Rhone, although vintages such as 1977 were characterized by a lack of ripening.

H

hard: Wines with abrasive, astringent tannins or high acidity are said to be hard. Young vintages of Rhone wines can be hard, but they should never be harsh.

harsh: If a wine is too hard it is said to be harsh. Harshness in a wine, young or old, is a flaw.

hedonistic: Certain styles of wine are meant to be inspected; they are introspective and intellectual wines. Others are designed to provide sheer delight, joy, and euphoria. Hedonistic wines can be criticized because in one sense they provide so much ecstasy that they can be called obvious, but in essence, they are totally gratifying wines meant to fascinate and enthral pleasure at its best.

herbaceous: Many wines have a distinctive herbal smell that is generally said to be herbaceous. Specific herbal smells can be of thyme, lavender, rosemary, oregano, fennel, or basil and are common in Rhone wines.

herbes de Provence: Provence is known for the wild herbs that grow prolifically through- out the region. These include lavender, thyme, sage, rosemary, and oregano. It is not just an olfactory fancy to smell many of these herbs in Rhone Valley wines, particularly those made in the south.

hollow: Also known as shallow, hollow wines are diluted and lack depth and concentration.

honeyed: A common personality trait of specific white Rhone wines, a honeyed wine is one that has the smell and taste of bee's honey.

hot: Rather than meaning that the temperature of the wine is too warm to drink, hot denotes that the wine is too high in alcohol and therefore leaves a burning sensation in the back of the throat when swallowed. Wines with alcohol levels in excess of 14.5% often taste hot if the requisite depth of fruit is not present.

I

inox vats: This is the French term for stainless steel vats that are used for both fermentation and storage of wine.

intensity: Intensity is one of the most desirable traits of a high-quality wine. Wines of great intensity must also have balance. They should never be heavy or cloying. Intensely concentrated great wines are alive, vibrant, aromatic, layered, and texturally compelling. Their intensity adds to their character, rather than detracting from it.

J

jammy: When wines have a great intensity of fruit from excellent ripeness they can be jammy, which is a very concentrated, flavorful wine with superb extract. In great vintages such as 1961, 1978, 1985, 1989, 1990, and 1995, some of the wines are so concentrated that they are said to be jammy.

K

Kisselguhr filtration system: This is a filtration system using diatomaceous earth as the filtering material, rather than cellulose, or in the past, before it was banned, asbestos.

L

leafy: A leafy character in a wine is similar to a herbaceous character only in that it refers to the smell of leaves rather than herbs. A wine that is too leafy is a vegetal or green wine.

lean: Lean wines are slim, rather streamlined wines that lack generosity and fatness but can still be enjoyable and pleasant.

lively: A synonym for fresh or exuberant, a lively wine is usually young wine with good acidity and a thirst-quenching personality.

long: A very desirable trait in any fine wine is that it be long in the mouth. Long (or length) relates to a wine's finish, meaning that after you swallow the wine, you sense its presence for a long time. (Thirty seconds to several minutes is great length.) In a young wine, the difference between something good and something great is the length of the wine.

lush: Lush wines are velvety, soft, richly fruity wines that are both concentrated and fat. A lush wine can never be an astringent or hard wine.

M

massive: In great vintages where there is a high degree of ripeness and superb concentration, some wines can turn out to be so big, full-bodied, and rich that they are called massive. A great wine such as the 1961 or 1990 Hermitage La Chapelle is a textbook example of a massive wine.

meaty: A chewy, fleshy wine is also said to be meaty.

monocepage: This term describes a wine made totally of one specific varietal.

monopole: Used to denote a vineyard owned exclusively by one proprietor, the word monopole appears on the label of a wine made from such a vineyard.

morsellated: Many vineyards are fragmented, with multiple growers owning a portion of the same vineyard. Such a vineyard is often referred to as a morsellated vineyard.

mouth-filling: Big, rich, concentrated wines that are filled with fruit extract and are high in alcohol and glycerin are wines that tend to texturally fill the mouth. A mouth-filling wine is also a chewy, fleshy, fat wine.

musty: Wines aged in dirty barrels or unkept cellars or exposed to a bad cork take on a damp, musty character that is a flaw.

N

nose: The general smell and aroma of a wine as sensed through one's nose and olfactory senses is often called the wine's nose.

O

oaky: Many red Rhone wines are aged from 6 months to 30 months in various sizes of oak barrels. At some properties, a percentage of the oak barrels may be new, and these barrels impart a toasty, vanillin flavour and smell to the wine. If the wine is not rich and concentrated, the barrels can overwhelm the wine, making it taste overly oaky. Where the wine is rich and concentrated and the winemaker has made a judicious use of barrels, however, the results are a wonderful marriage of fruit and oak.

off: If a wine is not showing its true character, or is flawed or spoiled in some way, it is said to be "off."

overripe: An undesirable characteristic; grapes left too long on the vine become too ripe, lose their acidity, and produce wines that are heavy and balance. This can happen frequently in the hot viticultural areas of the Rhone Valley if the growers harvest too late.

oxidized: If a wine has been excessively exposed to air during either its making or aging, the wine loses freshness and takes on a stale, old smell and taste. Such a wine is said to be oxidized.

P

peppery: A peppery quality to a wine is usually noticeable in many Rhone wines that have an aroma of black or white pepper and a pungent flavour.

perfumed: This term usually is more applicable to fragrant, aromatic white wines than to red wines. However, some of the dry white wines (particularly Condrieu) and sweet white wines can have a strong perfumed smell.

pigéage: A winemaking technique of punching down the cap of grape skins that forms during the beginning of the wine's fermentation. This is done several times a day, occasionally more frequently, to extract colour, flavour, and tannin from the fermenting juice.

plumy: Rich, concentrated wines can often have the smell and taste of ripe plums. When they do, the term plumy is applicable.

ponderous: Ponderous is often used as a synonym for massive, but in my usage a massive wine is simply a big, rich, very concentrated wine with balance, whereas a ponderous wine is a wine that has become heavy and tiring to drink.

precocious: Wines that mature quickly are precocious. However the term also applies to wines that may last and evolve gracefully over a long period of time, but taste as if they are aging quickly because of their tastiness and soft, early charms.

pruney: Wines produced from grapes that are overripe take on the character of prunes. Pruney wines are flawed wines.

R

raisiny: Late-harvest wines that are meant to be drunk at the end of a meal can often be slightly raisiny, which in some ports and sherries is desirable. However, a raisiny quality is a major flaw in a dinner wine.

rich: Wines that are high in extract, flavour, and intensity of fruit.

ripe: A wine is ripe when its grapes have reached the optimum level of maturity. Less than fully mature grapes produce wines that are underripe, and overly mature grapes produce wines that are overripe.

round: A very desirable character of wines, roundness occurs in fully mature wines that have lost their youthful, astringent tannins, and also in young wines that have soft tannins and low acidity.

S

savory: A general descriptive term that denotes that the wine is round, flavorful, and interesting to drink. shallow: A weak, feeble, watery or diluted wine lacking concentration is said to be shallow.

sharp: An undesirable trait, sharp wines are bitter and unpleasant with hard, pointed edges.

silky: A synonym for velvety or lush, silky wines are soft, sometimes fat, but never hard or angular.

smoky: Some wines, either because of the soil or because of the barrels used to age the wine, have a distinctive smoky character. Cote Rotie and Hermitage often have a roasted or smoky quality.

soft: A soft wine is one that is round and fruity, low in acidity, and has an absence of aggressive, hard tannins.

spicy: Wines often smell quite spicy with aromas of pepper, cinnamon, and other well-known spices. These pungent aromas are usually lumped together and called spicy.

stale: Dull, heavy wines that are oxidized or lack balancing acidity for freshness are called stale.

stalky: A synonym for vegetal, but used more frequently to denote that the wine has probably had too much contact with the stems, resulting in a green, vegetal, or stalky character to the wine.

supple: A supple wine is one that is soft, lush, velvety, and very attractively round and tasty. It is a highly desirable characteristic because it suggests that the wine is harmonious.

T

tannic: The tannins of a wine, which are extracted from the grape skins and stems, are, along with a wine's acidity and alcohol, its lifeline. Tannins give a wine firmness and some roughness when young, but gradually fall away and dissipate. A tannic wine is one that is young and unready to drink.

tart: Sharp, acidic, lean, unripe wines are called tart. In general, a wine that is tart is not pleasurable.

thick: Rich, ripe, concentrated wines that are low in acidity are often said to be thick.

thin: A synonym for shallow; it is an undesirable characteristic for a wine to be thin, meaning that it is watery, lacking in body, and just diluted.

tightly knit: Young wines that have good acidity levels, good tannin levels, and are well made are called tightly knit, meaning they have yet to open up and develop.

toasty: A smell of grilled toast can often be found in wines because the barrels the wines are aged in are charred or toasted on the inside.

tobacco: Some red wines have the scent of fresh tobacco. It is a distinctive and wonderful smell in wine.

troncais oak: This type of oak comes from the forest of Troncais in central France.

U

unctuous: Rich, lush, intense wines with layers of concentrated, soft, velvety fruit are said to be unctuous.

V

vegetal: An undesirable characteristic, wines that smell and taste vegetal are usually made from unripe grapes. In some wines, a subtle vegetable garden smell is pleasant and adds complexity, but if it is the predominant character, it is a major flaw.

velvety: A textural description and synonym for lush or silky, a velvety wine is a rich, soft, smooth wine to taste. It is a very desirable characteristic.

viscous: Viscous wines tend to be relatively concentrated, fat, almost thick wines with a great density of fruit extract, plenty of glycerin, and high alcohol content. If they have balancing acidity, they can be tremendously flavourful and exciting wines. If they lack acidity, they are often flabby and heavy.

volatile: A volatile wine is one that smells of vinegar as a result of an excessive amount of acetic bacteria present. It is a seriously flawed wine.

W

woody: When a wine is overly oaky it is often said to be woody. Oakiness in a wine's bouquet and taste is good up to a point. Once past that point, the wine is woody and its fruity qualities are masked by excessive oak aging.

www.ingramcontent.com/pod-product-compliance
Lightning Source LLC
Chambersburg PA
CBHW060810050426
42449CB00008B/1616